SUSANNA

SUSANNA

by Rebecca Lamar Harmon

MOTHER OF THE WESLEYS

SUSANNA WESLEY   ARTIST UNKNOWN
COURTESY OF EPWORTH PRESS, LONDON

ABINGDON PRESS • *Nashville*

SUSANNA, MOTHER OF THE WESLEYS

Library of Congress Catalog Card Number: 68-11463

ISBN 0-687-40766-4

MANUFACTURED BY THE PARTHENON PRESS AT
NASHVILLE, TENNESSEE, UNITED STATES OF AMERICA

TO THE LADY OF THE PARSONAGE
WHEREVER SHE MAY BE

THE EPWORTH WESLEY FAMILY [1]

NAME	BIRTHPLACE	BORN	DIED	BURIAL PLACE	AGE
Samuel Wesley, Sr. [2]	Whitchurch	late in 1662	4/25/1735	Epworth Churchyard	73
Susanna	London	1/20/1669	7/23/1742	Bunhill Fields, London	73
		CHILDREN			
1. Samuel, Jr.	London	2/10/1690	11/6/1739	Tiverton	49
2. Susanna	South Ormsby	1691	4/1693	South Ormsby	Infant
3. Emilia (Harper)	"	1/1692	1771	London	79
4. Annesley ⎱ twins	"	1694	1/31/1695	South Ormsby	Infants
5. Jedediah ⎰					
6. Susanna (Ellison)	"	1695	12/7/1764	London	69
7. Mary (Whitelamb) [3]	"	1696	11/1734	Wroote	38
8. Mehetabel (Wright)	Epworth	1697	3/21/1750	London	53
9. Not known whether boy or girl	"	1698	soon died	Epworth	Infant

NAME	BIRTHPLACE	BORN	DIED	BURIAL PLACE	AGE
10. John	Epworth	5/18/1699	soon died	Epworth	Infant
11. Benjamin	,,	1700	,,	,,	,,
12 & 13. Unnamed twins	,,	5/17/1701	,,	,,	,,
14. Anne (Lambert)	,,	1702	?		
15. John	,,	6/17/1703	3/2/1791	City Road, London	87
16. Son smothered by nurse	,,	5/8/05	5/30/05	Epworth	Infant
17. Martha (Hall)	,,	5/8/1706	7/19/1791	City Road, London	85
18. Charles	,,	12/18/1707	3/29/1788	Marylebone, ,,	80
19. Kezziah	,,	3/1709	3/9/1741	London	32

1. Data assembled chiefly from Stevenson's **Memorials of the Wesley Family** and Adam Clarke's **Memoirs of the Wesley Family.**
2. Stevenson gives 12/17/1662 as Samuel Wesley's birth date, but according to Kirk, the parish register of Whitchurch gives 12/17/1662 as the date of his baptism.
3. Stevenson lists Mary Wesley's place of birth as Epworth in 1696, but Dr. Frank Baker's more recent research establishes 1697 as the date of arrival of the Wesley's at Epworth, so Mary must have been born at South Ormsby.

FOREWORD

In presenting this book I wish to picture, from the point of view of a woman of the twentieth century, a very remarkable lady of the eighteenth. Susanna Wesley—although she would have been the last person to realize it—has had a profound influence upon her own country and other nations as well.

Her life, like any other, must always be viewed against the background of the time in which she lived; otherwise she will be entirely misunderstood.

Her life accomplishment was effected mainly within the

narrow circle of a home in a remote and uncongenial swamp of Lincolnshire. Her activities were restricted to her family and her husband's parish. Yet she gave to the world two geniuses of the first rank: John, founder of Methodism, and Charles, one of the greatest hymn writers of all time.

She was a superb teacher, among her other qualities. And since the secret of the perfect way to raise children has not yet been discovered, perhaps the method of this pre-Victorian mother holds something of value for parents of our modern day.

The picture here given of eighteenth-century English society may even be admonitory in its resemblance to our time. Be that as it may, I hope that there will be entertainment and instruction in the story of this unusual lady in whose stimulating company it has been my good fortune to live these many months.

Were it possible, I should like to express my appreciation to the late Dr. Elmer T. Clark who opened to me unusual Wesleyana sources. Thanks are due also to Miss Elizabeth Royer, librarian of the theology library of Emory University, and to her staff, for their consistent kindness during my hours of research there; and to Dr. Maldwyn Edwards whose balanced evaluation of each member of the Epworth family has steadied my judgment at many points. I remember also with great appreciation the gracious hospitality of Mr. and Mrs. Horace Burrell at the old Epworth Rectory which, in imagination, I could people again with its illustrious inmates of two centuries ago. I am deeply grateful to Dr. Frank Baker who generously permitted me to use hitherto unpublished data—the result of his personal research—which unquestionably establishes the paternity of Hetty Wesley's first child. Most of all, I should thank my husband, Bishop Nolan B. Harmon, without whose encouragement and advice I should never have ventured beyond the first page.

REBECCA LAMAR HARMON

CONTENTS

1
MEETING SUSANNA.................................13

2
THE ANNESLEYS AND THE WESLEYS................. 23

3
THE ENGLAND OF SUSANNA'S TIME................. 31

4
LIFE AT EPWORTH 40

5
SUSANNA AS MOTHER AND TEACHER 55

6
OLD JEFFREY, THE GHOST 66

7
SUSANNA IN THE PARISH 74

8
EPWORTH AND WROOT........................... 85

9
THE DAUGHTERS 102

10
HETTY.....................................117

11
THE SONS..................................138

12
SUSANNA AT THE FOUNDERY 151

SAYINGS OF SUSANNA 165

NOTES 167

BIBLIOGRAPHY..............................170

INDEX....................................173

SPITAL YARD, A TINY BUT RESPECTABLE STREET, WHERE SUSANNA WAS BORN.

1
MEETING SUSANNA

The parson's wife found herself quite weary as she alighted from the lumbering coach before the door of the Epworth parsonage. It had been a long and exhausting journey from their former parish of South Ormsby, in spite of the fact that the trip was just across the county. There was no road worthy of the name within forty miles of Epworth, so they jolted endlessly through the fields. More than once their coach had to be pulled out of deep ruts by draft animals from neighboring farms, and each time the children became thoroughly chilled as they waited outside in the cold wind. Too, Mrs. Wesley was in constant fear of highwaymen who were terrorizing the countryside in all directions, though there would certainly be little to gain from the debt-ridden family of a country rector.[1]

In spite of her shabby cloak and her outmoded bonnet, there was an air of quiet elegance about this English gentlewoman as she walked with head held high toward the entrance of her new home. A pretty face looked out from behind that bonnet and its little chin spelled determination in every line. The Reverend Samuel Wesley lifted down their children, one by one, from the coach, four of them—there would be a fifth before the year was out. The door opened in welcome to the new rector and his brood, his wife ushered the children inside in orderly precision, and thus began a pastorate which was to last for thirty-nine years.

Oh, Susanna! Beautiful, indomitable Susanna! Little did you dream what you started when you left your father's sheltered home on the arm of the diminutive Reverend Samuel Wesley! For partly because of circumstance, and partly, we must verily believe, because the hand of God was in it, this parsonage at Epworth was destined to become the most celebrated in all English history, and Susanna became the mother of the tremendous little preacher who rocked the world.

Mrs. Wesley had small opportunity to rest from the rigors of her journey. Indeed, she would class such a procedure as self-indulgence since there was so much to do to set their new establishment in order.

A tour of inspection proved the new home to be a great improvement over the "mean cot, composed of reeds and clay," as her husband once described their former rectory at South Ormsby. The Epworth parsonage consisted of "five baies, built all of timber and plaister, and covered with straw thatche, the whole building being contrived into three stories, and disposed in seven chief rooms—a kitchinge, a hall, a parlour, a butterie, and three large upper rooms, and some others of common use; and also a little garden, empailed betwine the stone wall and the south." [2] There was "one barn of six baies, built all of timber and clay walls and covered with straw thatche, with outshotts about it and free house therebye." There were a dovecot and a hemp-kiln. Altogether the "scite" of the rectory contained about three acres. "Plenty of space for the children," thought Susanna hopefully.

Surely the Wesleys were better off with the new living of two hundred pounds[3]—a far cry from the thirty pounds of South Ormsby. But they were in debt. The stipend they received at South Ormsby, though doubled by Samuel's writings, had never fully met the expenses of their rapidly growing family. Now, even the new salary would not be nearly enough, for additional furnishings must be provided for the larger house, there were taxes incident to establishing them in a new living, and a yearly amount must be sent to Samuel's mother to keep her from starving. "Farming on the glebe land (parish church property) might eke out the difference," thought Susanna to herself.

Few ministers' wives have ever looked out upon a more desolate landscape than did Susanna as she viewed the environs of their new rectory for the first time—dreary fenlands interspersed with narrow ditches, a scattering of village dwellings, the church across the field a little way, and a few trees bending in a relentless wind. "A flat malarial land of reed and rush where north winds sweep and an angry sea drives far inland, and where morning ever steps with misty feet and evening follows with sallow-rifted glooms." [4] Such was Lincolnshire when the Wesleys arrived.

The tiny, low-lying "island" of Axholme, surrounded by four rivers, the Trent, the Don, the Tarne, and the Idle, was the site of Mr. Wesley's parish. Though many years before the Wesleys' arrival the Dutchman Cornelius Vermuyden had been commissioned to drain the swamps and turn them into fertile farm land, the rivers still overflowed the low country-side at times, adding to the general inaccessibility of the place.

Lucky for Susanna that first day that she did not fully realize the nature of her husband's parishioners. These brutish fenland folk were the product of their environment. They had little contact with the outside world and no education to speak of and so viewed with high suspicion any intrusion either of new people or fresh ideas.

Picture a community where the best of the citizenry could read but falteringly, where there was no newspaper, no library, mail but once a week, and an insularity almost complete, and it is easy to understand why their "manners were coarse and vicious," why "fights were their favorite diversion," and their thinking narrow and mulish.

But this was no ordinary couple—these Wesleys who had been sent to minister to the Lincolnshire parish. They were well-educated, cultured people, each from a long line of noble ancestry. Furthermore, their dedication to their sacred calling was complete, else how could they have labored so long and so faithfully in this desolate spot so different from the London of Susanna's upbringing?

Young Mrs. Wesley was never given to vain repining over the past—the present with its many duties was too demanding for that. But during those early days at Epworth there must have been an undercurrent of sadness to her thoughts. Her father had died shortly before their arrival—that handsome, commanding figure, Dr. Samuel Annesley, around whom the life of her childhood so happily revolved. She could be for-given a few nostalgic pangs as her mind reverted to him and all the associations of her early youth.

She had been brought up in an English parsonage where children were counted by the dozen—there were two dozen Annesleys or a quarter of a hundred, Dr. Manton who baptized

Susanna could not remember which. Susanna was the youngest.

Too little is known of Susanna's childhood. She was born in London on January 20, 1669. By the time she came upon the scene her father, being a Nonconformist, had been forced out of his important Anglican parish of St. Giles, one of the largest in London. Dr. Annesley later became the minister of the Puritan meetinghouse of Little St. Helen's where he developed a large and influential congregation. Spital Yard, a tiny but respectable street between Spital Square and Bishopgate St., London, was the location of Dr. Annesley's parsonage during his pastorate at Little St. Helen's. It is here that Susanna was born and spent her youth.

On one occasion Susanna spoke of being preserved from ill accidents, once from violent death during her childhood; but there are practically no incidents recorded about her early youth. We know that her home life was a happy one with plenty of wholesome fun.

Four years before her birth, the Great Plague which had its beginning in St. Giles, her father's former parish, had ravaged London. Many were the stories she heard of thousands who died of that disease within a few days. People who had witnessed the London fire one year later could give her firsthand accounts of its destruction. When Susanna was growing up, London was in the exciting process of reconstruction. The plague had taught the city some lessons in cleanliness. Wider streets and better houses were laid out by Robert Hooke, and doubtless Susanna herself watched the building of St. Paul's Cathedral, the work of the famous Sir Christopher Wren.

The records about Susanna's brothers and sisters are equally scant. If the Annesley family followed the usual pattern of that day, a goodly number of the children must have died before they reached maturity. We know that the oldest named Samuel died early; that another son, given the same name, was trained as a merchant; that he left his family to go to India where he became quite wealthy; that he made many promises of financial help to Susanna's family but failed to keep them; that he died in India quite mysteriously.

There were handsome daughters in the Annesley home: Judith and Anne and Sarah and Elizabeth. There was also a younger son, Benjamin, who became the executor of his father's will.

Susanna, so the record has it, was a pretty girl, the most beautiful of her family, slim and graceful, "retaining her figure to old age." She was cultured and gracious, "with some measure of wit," though she was reputed to be of more serious temperament than her gay and rollicking sisters. Susanna was of an even disposition, with a "deep and natural piety" which she is said to have inherited from her mother. In a letter written to her son John in later years she says that early in life she made it a rule "never to spend more time in any matter of mere recreation in one day" than she "spent in private religious duties." But with all her piety, this daughter of the parsonage was strong in her opinions and fearless in sticking to them.

Dr. Annesley kept a sort of "open house" for Nonconformist pastors of London and vicinity as well as young students of that persuasion. Among the many visitors to the hospitable house in Spital Yard was Samuel Wesley, a student at the Reverend Edward Veal's Dissenting Academy and a son and grandson of Nonconformist parsons.[5] It is here that he and Susanna met when quite young. It is worthy of mention also that John Dunton, Samuel Wesley's eccentric publisher, who married Susanna's sister Elizabeth, was a frequent visitor at the Annesley parsonage.

Susanna, of course, never went to college. In her day woman's education was "sadly to seek," as Trevelyan put it. There were a few girls' boarding schools of poor quality, but, generally speaking, even a high-born lady's library was limited to a prayerbook and a collection of recipes. That Susanna received a good education, however, is attested by the classic simplicity of her writing and her ability to hold her own in the learned theological discussions that constituted the table talk in homes such as Dr. Annesley's. Her father recognized the intellectual acumen of his favorite daughter and took a part in her education.

It is quite likely that Susanna had a knowledge of French. Some historians state that she was well versed in Latin and Greek; but this is highly improbable, for her letters to her sons at Oxford are completely devoid of classical phrases, as are their replies. The letters to their father, however, are heavily embroidered with Latin and Greek. Furthermore, in a letter to his son Samuel at Westminster School, Samuel Wesley, Sr. urges Sammy to write freely about his inmost thoughts:

"I will promise you so much secrecy that even your mother shall know nothing but what you have a mind she should; for which reason it may be convenient you should write to me still in Latin"—which, incidentally, proves something else about the status of women in the eighteenth century beside the quality of their education.

Unquestionably, though, Susanna's was a "well-stored" mind and a logical one, and her exercise of it was to have great effect in fashioning the mold of the people called Methodists.

By no stretch of the imagination could Susanna ever have been called a mystic. Devout and good she was from childhood, but common sense was always dominant, especially in her religion. In writing to John at Oxford she once said: "I take à Kempis to have been an honest, weak man, who had more zeal than knowledge, by his condemning all mirth or pleasure as sinful or useless. . . ." And again: "Let everyone enjoy the present hour. Age and successive troubles are sufficient to convince any man that it is much wiser and safer to deprecate great afflictions than to pray for them, and that our Lord knew what was in man when he directed us to pray: 'Lead us not into temptation.' " Again, in her *Meditations* she writes: "Religion is not to be confined to the church or closet, nor exercised only in prayer and meditation, but everywhere I am in His presence." "Hers was a religion of enlightened principle, rather than transient emotion." [6]

"A theologian in short dresses," William Fitchett calls Susanna, and well he may. Before she was thirteen years of age she had carefully sifted the tenets of her father's belief. She had weighed them in the balance against the doctrines of the Established Church and had decided in favor of the Church. Samuel Wesley before ending his Academy days had made a similar decision. He, too, was the son of a Dissenting clergyman, and what was more natural than that he and the beautiful Susanna should become attracted to each other!

A quaint courtship this must have been, these two serious young people, withdrawn a bit from the merry group in the rectory parlor, in earnest discussion of deep religious principles. Samuel was able to lead his future wife out of the mazes of Socinianism in which she was then wandering and to help her establish a firm and lasting belief in the Trinity.

And what of this young cleric who was to be Susanna's life companion?

Historians are at variance as to the date of Samuel Wesley's birth, but it is fairly well established that he was born in November, 1662. This is substantiated by his baptismal record, found in the church at Whitchurch and dated December 17, 1662. He, too, came out of a Nonconformist parsonage—a parsonage full of children and poverty—stricken like the homes of most of the Dissenting parsons when the Act of Uniformity deprived them of their living. The names of but three of the Wesley children beside Samuel are known: Timothy, Elizabeth, and Matthew.

Samuel's father, John, persecuted and driven from pillar to post, died of a broken heart at the time Samuel was attend-

ing Dorchester free school, but his mother managed somehow
to keep him there till he finished his course. No Dissenter was
permitted by law to attend a university in England, so with a
thirty-pound yearly stipend from the Dissenters' fund, Samuel
entered Mr. Veal's Dissenting Academy in London, a school of
high academic standards. After two years he transferred to
Mr. Morton's Academy, an equally good school. Among his
fellow students there were John Dunton, his future brother-
in-law, and Daniel Defoe. It was during this period that he
heard some of the most noted of the Nonconformist preachers,
including John Bunyan.

Samuel Wesley proved a fine student and a young man of
excellent character. It was at Mr. Morton's School that he
undertook a thorough study of the Dissenters' beliefs and as
a result decided with finality that his conscience would not
permit him to follow the convictions of his father. To his
credit it is recorded that he discharged all financial obligations
to the Nonconformists by means of a small legacy he inherited,
then turned his face toward the university and ministry in the
Established Church.

Well he knew that his Dissenting mother would be violently
opposed to this change of allegiance, so he slipped out from
home one August morning in 1683, and with forty-five
shillings in his pocket and his knapsack on his back, set out on
foot for Oxford, the impregnable citadel of English con-
servatism. His father and grandfather had gone to Oxford.
Why not he? The fact that his widowed mother had not a
farthing more for his education deterred him not a whit. So, a
pauper scholaris, the lowest of the four conditions of member-
ship, he entered Exeter College of the great university. One
crown was the sum total of outside help he received during
his entire five-year stay at Oxford, but he was able to defray
his expenses by the strictest economy in food, fuel, and cloth-
ing, by serving other students and tutoring them, and by his
pen. His only luxury was his trusty pipe.

In spite of his demanding schedule he found time to minister to the prisoners in the Castle at Oxford—a service which was later repeated by his sons during their student days.

Samuel's first book was a collection of poems under the odd title of "Maggots." It began with these revealing lines:

> In his own defence the author writes
> Because when this foul maggot bites
> He ne'er can rest in quiet. . . .

This little volume, light and witty in character, was published by John Dunton at the Black Raven printing establishment in London in 1685, while Samuel was still a student at Oxford. The "maggot" continued to bite him for the rest of his life for he was determined to be a poet of the first rank—an ambition which was never realized even in the opinion of his admiring sons. "Maggots" was to be followed by many more writings of a serious nature as Samuel's reputation as a scholar increased.

This husband of Susanna's was cast in no commonplace mold. He was small in stature but with strength of purpose out of all proportion to his size. His body was toughened by privation and his will was equally inflexible. He was peppery and quick-tempered, in contrast to Susanna's even disposition; tact was completely absent from his makeup. Samuel Wesley was never practical; indeed, he has even been called irresponsible by some historians who thoroughly disliked him. He was, in fact, strikingly like David Copperfield's friend Mr. Micawber. But for culture, industry, devotion to his calling and his family, and for downright courage, Samuel Wesley should receive a high rating.

Poverty stalked the life of the little rector from birth until his last hour, but he was never daunted by it.

Susanna and Samuel were married about 1689 when Susanna was nineteen or twenty and Samuel in his twenty-eighth year. It was a love match to the end of their lives together.

SAMUEL WESLEY ... WAS CAST
IN NO COMMONPLACE MOLD.

2
THE ANNESLEYS
and the WESLEYS

The unpardonable sin for any storyteller is to digress even
slightly from the unrolling of his tale. But it is also true that
most readers unconsciously place the characters on the page
before them in a contemporary setting and thus receive a
distorted image.

The period of 1669 to 1742 was a long time ago, and to
form a true picture of Susanna Wesley it is necessary to view
her against the background of her ancestry and the time in

which she lived. So, in fairness to this elect lady of an earlier
day, we shall try to place her in the proper frame.

Adam Clarke, meticulous historian that he was, traces Susanna Annesley's lineage back beyond the advent of William
the Conqueror. For our purpose it is sufficient to go back no
further than her grandfather John Anslye, a British preacher,
and Judith his wife, godly people who dedicated their only son
at his birth "for the work of the ministry." Appropriately, they
named him Samuel after the prophet of old who received a
similar consecration. John Anslye died when his son was four
years old, and Samuel was carefully reared in a pious tradition by his mother.

Susanna's maternal grandfather John White, a Welsh Puritan, was a distinguished lawyer and for many years a member
of Parliament from Southwark. He demonstrated the strength
of his character when, as chairman of a committee from the
House of Commons to investigate the immoralities of the
clergy, he made a fearless exposé of his scandalous findings.
Perhaps it is from this ancestor that Susanna inherited the
merciless logic of her reasoning—a quality she passed on in
abundant measure to her famous son, John.

Susanna's father, Samuel Annesley, was a born leader. Tall
and handsome, he radiated a certain exuberance of good health
and looked every inch the aristocrat that he was. He entered
Oxford at the age of fifteen and was outstanding for his goodness and industry rather than for his intellectual acumen—but
how his fellows followed him! Those who knew him loved
him devotedly.

In due time, about 1644, Samuel Annesley completed the
preparation for his beloved calling, was ordained and assigned
to his first parish. Here began a long series of persecutions
and hardships that persisted for many years.

From the start, his parishioners in his first settled charge at
Cliffe resented him bitterly. They were used to a carefree,
laissez-faire rector who winked at their riotous living. And

now comes a mere fledgling of a preacher to chastise them
for their drunkenness and other excesses. They went at him
with stones, even threatened his life, but the winsome goodness of his personality finally took over and made remarkable
changes in this worldly parish.

But there were graver troubles in store for the young
cleric. England was then in the throes of a bitter conflict,
both in politics and religion, between the Church and the
Dissenters. The extremists on the Church side wanted an
absolute monarchy in the realm and an ironclad episcopacy in
the Church; the Dissenters demanded a limited monarchy in
the realm and a Church government by presbyters or by a
union of presbyters and bishops. As the outcome of this struggle, King Charles I was beheaded (January 30, 1649) and
Oliver Cromwell was declared Protector. Annesley, like many
a Nonconformist, was probably more Royalist than Roundhead
in his political sympathies. Certainly he disapproved heartily
of the execution of King Charles, but he did not hesitate to lash
out against evils in either group and so found himself constantly in hot water.

As early as his first pastorate he was called upon to preach
before the House of Commons, and during a fiery discourse
he antagonized the Royalists, still in the ascendency at that
time, by an indirect but unmistakable censure of the king.
Later on when the Puritans came to power he publicly called
Oliver Cromwell "the arrantest hypocrite the Church of Christ
was ever pestered with," and for this he was punished by being
ousted from one of the most important parishes in England
and transferred to the tiniest church in London (about 1650).

Oliver Cromwell, a ruthless ruler, did much for England in
the five years of his Protectorate. Under his strong hand the
country rose to heights of power and greatness. But in spite
of their prosperity the people were not happy. They were used
to a king, and a Puritan regime was too strict for most of
them. Richard Cromwell who succeeded his father was too

weak for the role he inherited and retired to the Continent.
Then on May 25, 1660, the fleet arrived at Dover bearing the
Merry Monarch, Prince Charles, returning from exile in
Holland. He disembarked amid great pomp and ceremony, and
England had a king again.

When the Dissenters saw that under the new regime the
Church party showed no sign of forming a union with them,
they appealed to the new king for discretionary powers in the
conduct of their ministry. After all, the Church of England
was Protestant, and therefore its clergy, the dissenting members stoutly maintained, were entitled to some latitude in the
use of the Prayer Book to conform to the dictates of their
consciences.

The king was well aware that the Dissenters had helped to
bring him back, so even before his actual return he made
favorable promises to them. On March 25, 1661, King Charles
II appointed a commission with equal representation from
both sides—eleven bishops and eleven Dissenting leaders, its
purpose being to resolve this whole matter. This commission
made some changes in the Prayer Book—the last changes
made to this present day—but the Church group was completely unyielding in its position. Again the Dissenters appealed
to the king; but they were dealing with a pleasure-loving
monarch who allowed the bishops to have their way.

From then on, stark tragedy moved nearer and nearer to
Nonconformists like Samuel Annesley. Early in 1662, the
legislature passed the Act of Uniformity whereby each minister
of the Establishment must promise, among other things, complete compliance with every word prescribed in the Book of
Common Prayer. This edict was considered by the Dissenters
"as wiping out all benefits of liberty of conscience that had
been theirs since the Reformation." Fall in line, the law
prescribed, or be ejected from your parish and preach no more
from any Anglican pulpit in England! The same Act applied

to all teachers and tutors under penalty of three months' imprisonment.

Again a group of the most eminent divines of London, Samuel Annesley among them, appealed to the king, and again they were overruled. In vain did Dr. Annesley's close relative, the Earl of Anglesea, plead with him to conform, promising the use of his vast influence for a place of high rank in the Church. Dr. Annesley remained firm.

And so on St. Bartholomew's Day, August 24, 1662, Samuel Annesley and two thousand of his fellow priests preached to their people for the last time and went out for conscience's sake, not knowing whither they went.

For the next ten years, there is little record of Dr. Annesley except that he lived in London. Then in 1672, when the Declaration of Indulgence eliminated for all Dissenters the possibility of legal prosecution, Dr. Annesley set up a "meeting house" in London called Little St. Helen's, which under his ministry became a large and influential church. He soon became a leader of the Puritans—a second St. Paul, they called him—helping to place Dissenting parsons, relieving their financial distress, and spending much time and energy upon young candidates for the ministry.

Dr. Annesley originally had a "good estate" which he devoted to charity. Perhaps it was during this trying period that his fortune disappeared. Many Nonconformist ministers upon their expulsion from their parishes were left with no source of livelihood whatever, and Dr. Annesley was always generous to a fault. Be that as it may, except for modest bequests to his son and his two unmarried daughters, his legacy was a mere shilling apiece to his children, and to Susanna he left his valuable papers and manuscripts.

It is a rather striking commentary on the magnanimity of Dr. Annesley that he never held it against his favorite daughter that she joined the Established Church, particularly when he himself paid such a heavy price for his nonconformity to that faith. Doubtless he thought her entitled to an independence of opinion equal to his own when she dissented from the Dissenters!

There were marked differences between the temperaments of Susanna and her father. He was a social type and strode through the streets of London without hat or coat even in the bitterest weather, with a greeting for all he met. Susanna was quiet and contemplative, more penetrating in intellect. She was slower in making up her mind but unwavering once that had been accomplished. Her father was quicker on decisions but more willing to compromise than his daughter.

As is characteristic of that period, Susanna's mother is given little space by the historians. A second wife, she is thought to have been the mother of all except the oldest of Dr. Annesley's large family. Her piety and human understanding are the qualities universally mentioned. Her daughter Elizabeth records the "united" efforts of her parents for their children's education. Perhaps Susanna's mother, too, kept school for her children and set the pattern which was to have such amazing results in the training of the founders of Methodism.

The Wesleys also were an old family. Genealogists trace the ancestors of Samuel Westley (as he was enrolled at Oxford) far back before the Normans conquered England and before surnames were used. The forbears of this family fought in the crusades. Edward, one of the ancestors, set out for Palestine with Sir James Douglas and intended to place the heart of Robert Bruce in the Holy Sepulcher; he was killed by the Saracens in 1340. It was this encounter that "entitles the Wesleys to use the scallop shell in the quarterings of their family arms." [1]

The Wesleys, like the Annesleys, seemed destined to live always in the thick of ecclesiastical conflict, and so it was with Bartholomew Wesley, the grandfather of Samuel. He was born in 1599, the same year as Oliver Cromwell, and was educated at Oxford in medicine and theology.

Bartholomew Wesley served acceptably in several parishes of his native Dorsetshire but like his grandson spoke out boldly whenever he saw fit, regardless of the consequences to his popularity. He joined the Puritans during the reign of Charles I. After the Restoration he was driven from his living and forbidden by the Five Mile Act to go within that distance of any former parish. From then on he practiced medicine for a livelihood, preaching whenever he could do so with safety.

His son, John Wesley, the father of Samuel, was another firebrand but of a different type from his father Bartholomew. He, too, was an Oxonian and won some fame in Oriental studies. He did not have regular ordination but was a sort of evangelist. Strangely enough, his way of preaching was strikingly similar to that of the Methodists under his famous grandson.

He accepted the living of Winterbourn, Whitchurch, under the "gathered church" which he had joined while at Oxford. This small living was insufficient for the needs of his family, so he maintained himself by teaching school.

When the bishop of Bristol questioned his right to preach without ordination according to the strict forms of the Church of England, Mr. John Wesley in true Wesley fashion defied him, and so effective was his preaching and so formidable his personality that the bishop decided not to "meddle" with him longer.

When the Restoration came, Mr. Wesley, too, dissented and even the bishop of Bristol could not save him. He moved from one church to another in rapid succession, with dire poverty his constant companion. In defiance of the Five Mile Act of 1665, he persisted in preaching. Four times he was imprisoned and was tormented each time. He died at the age of thirty-four, crushed in body and spirit. He is buried in the churchyard at Preston in an undistinguished grave, deprived, because of his dissent, of his proper place of burial in the church. His father Bartholomew, brokenhearted because of the persecution of his son, soon followed him in death.

"The opposition of Bartholomew and John Westley to the Common Prayer, and other ecclesiastical requisitions of the times, was more a protest against bigotry than bigotry itself; and by the progress of such dissent has the Anglo-Saxon mind reached its later and more forbearing liberality." [2]

"It cannot," observes Adam Clarke, "escape the notice and reflection of the reader, that Methodism, in its grand principles of economy, and the means by which they have been brought into action, has had its specific, healthy, though slowly vegetating, seeds in the original members of the Wesley family." [3]

The maternal grandfather of Samuel Wesley, strangely enough, bore the same name as Susanna's maternal grandfather, John White. He is commonly identified with a beloved rector of Trinity Church, Dorchester, who came to be affectionately called the "Patriarch of Dorchester" and one who helped to found Dorchester, Massachusetts, as an asylum for fugitives unable to conform to the discipline of the Church of England. Dr. Frank Baker, however, backed by eminent authority,[4] believes this identification to be erroneous, stating that there were at least three possible John Whites at this time. John Wesley himself seems to have been in error about the John White involved.

Samuel Wesley's mother was the niece of a celebrated clergyman, the Reverend Dr. Thomas Fuller, who was chaplain to King Charles II.

Little is told of Samuel's mother, but of her courage and resourcefulness we can be sure since she kept Samuel in school after his father's early death, in spite of her penury. She must have done the same for Samuel's brother Matthew who became an apothecary and surgeon with a lucrative practice in London. Samuel provided for her as long as she lived, and for a time she resided with the Epworth Wesleys in the rectory.

THE RELIGIOUS LIFE OF
ENGLAND WAS AT A LOW EBB.

3
THE ENGLAND
of SUSANNA'S TIME

England during Susanna Wesley's lifetime presented striking
contrasts. In some respects it was a golden age for English
genius. Newton and Boyle, Halley the astronomer, and the
early members of the Royal Society lent distinction in the
field of science. Hogarth was the realistic painter and carica-
turist of the period, with Gainsborough and Reynolds coming
on a bit later; Christopher Wren was the great architect,
Bentley the famous scholar and philosopher. Purcell and Hän-

del, who by this time had taken up his abode in England, were the musicians. Four years before Susanna's birth Milton gave to the world his *Paradise Lost,* and Dryden, Bunyan, Pope, Defoe, Addison and Steele, and Swift lent scintillating distinction in the field of letters.

Though experiments with machinery were in early process, the machine age had not yet made its real appearance; the English craftsman still took infinite pride in his handiwork. Chippendale and, a bit later, Adam brought the designing of furniture to a perfection of beauty which has scarcely been approached since. The manor houses of this era were large and elegant, built on lines of classic simplicity. Within there were art objects of great beauty, Jacobean paneling and handsome furniture. Rugs were now replacing the unsanitary rushes of former days. These rugs were imported from Turkey or Persia or could even be furnished by English weavers.

During the reign of Queen Anne, with Marlborough to win the battles, Britain was fast taking the lead in European civilization. The little island was pushing out its borders in colonization, and while it was to lose the American colonies in 1776, before the century ended Canada and India came to be added to its territory, won at but little cost; Australia was literally "plucked from the sea," as Trevelyan has it, by Captain Cook. Overseas trade was growing by leaps and bounds and the British navy with it, thus enhancing the power and prestige of the country.

In song and story the rural Englishman of Susanna's time is pictured as a happy, hearty individual, content with the independence of his life as a small farmer, or as a craftsman proud of his accomplishment with his own hands. These simple people were satisfied with the homely pleasures common to village life—or so they are pictured.

But there was a contrasting side to English life of that period. The court of Charles II, during whose reign Susanna was born, was a maze of corruption from which the country did not fully recover for a century after his reign. There was sensual dissipation of every sort. Drunkenness was the arch sin of the land; mistresses abounded, and the women were so immoral that there was a saying that a man was almost afraid to select a wife. Court ladies had beautiful clothes and elegant manners, but they knew how to curse and even to spit, and it was a common custom at Court for gentlemen to sit on the ladies' beds while they sipped their morning chocolate.

London, for all its fine houses, was filthy and ill-lighted. After dark, buckets of refuse were emptied from garret windows with no regard for those passing below. Thievery abounded.

Though there was great respect for learning in that day, poor transportation made it almost impossible for scholars like the Reverend Samuel Wesley to procure books. Rigid censorship was abolished just before the beginning of the eighteenth century, but the number of printing presses was very limited; nothing was published outside London and the universities. Many of the lords could barely sign their names, and the common people had practically no education. News circulated mostly in newsletters written by hand in London and sent out to towns and villages to be passed around. It is easy to see, therefore, why the Sunday sermon was so important: there was a dearth of books and news.

In the cities this situation was somewhat remedied by the advent of the Coffee Houses which, from the reign of Charles II to the time of the early Georges, were centers of social life in London and in other cities. The East India Company had by this time brought in tea and coffee, and nothing stronger was served in these gathering places. Furthermore, the Coffee Houses were much less expensive than modern clubs and quite democratic in their clientele. Since there were few means of disseminating news, the Coffee Houses filled that function. Most Londoners had their favorite house and could be found there at certain hours. There was a Coffee House frequented by the Whigs, another by the dandies of the day; still another by the clergy, another by men of letters, etc. Lloyd's Coffee House became the center for businessmen interested in news of shipping. The first Mr. Lloyd was a Coffee House keeper during the reign of Queen Anne. So began Lloyd's of London, one of the most famous insurance companies of the world.

Samuel Wesley in his younger days met with the other editors of the *Athenian Gazette* at Smith's Coffee House, George Yard. On one such occasion, a boisterous fellow kept swearing in loud tones audible to the whole room. In true Wesley fashion Samuel called for a waiter and instructed him to carry to the man a glass of water to wash out his mouth. The man became enraged and would have done bodily harm to Mr. Wesley but was restrained. Years later in St. James's Park, a stranger approached Samuel Wesley and introduced himself as the man he had reproved long ago in the Coffee House. "Since that time, sir," said he, "I thank God, I have feared an oath, and everything that is offensive to the Divine Majesty; and as I have a perfect recollection of you, I rejoice at seeing you, and could not refrain from expressing my gratitude to God and you." [1]

At the time of Susanna Wesley, the idea of a balanced diet was unknown; the majority of the nation is said to have lived almost entirely on oats, rye, and barley. Lack of proper medical care and unsanitary methods accounted for an enormous death rate, exceeding the birthrate. Smallpox carried off one thirteenth of the population until Jenner discovered vaccination, though it should be mentioned that in early 1722, Lady Mary Montagu brought to England from Turkey a form of inoculation against that dread disease.

Actually, the peasantry had seen little change in their way of living in a hundred years. Theirs was a life of drudgery, with wakes and fairs almost their sole diversion. Little children were put to work beside their mothers when they were as young as four or five years old, especially in the new and growing spinning industry. The Government did nothing for the education of the poor, so most of the villagers were illiterate. Even if they had known how to read and write, newspapers or magazines were too scarce to inform them about national affairs. Each village was a separate entity, and its inhabitants were satisfied to build their lives entirely around it, and their mental and spiritual horizons were correspondingly narrow.

In trying to form a picture of a woman's life in the time of Susanna Wesley, any twentieth-century woman would be curious to know what sort of help this mother of the eighteenth century had in giving birth to nineteen children in twenty-one years. But alas! such a subject in that day was highly indelicate. Indeed, in Mrs. Wesley's time the mere idea of putting into print instructions for midwives was considered immodest.

If only Susanna Wesley had been as chatty in her letters as Pepys was in his Diary, we would know much more about life in an English rectory generally and at the Epworth parsonage in particular. But family doings were evidently deemed by Mrs. Wesley too trivial to write about, with the result that much that might have been most interesting Wesleyana never was set down at all.

Susanna Wesley was delivered of all her babies by a midwife. We know that Samuel, Jr.'s birth was a difficult one and that Charles came prematurely, but other than that we know nothing of Susanna's many *accouchements*. Her husband Samuel, in a letter to the archbishop, lists among *his* misfortunes "one child at least *per annum* and my wife sick for half that time." We must remember in this connection that at that time asepsis and anesthesia were unknown.

As early as 1567, midwives were required to be licensed by the bishop, but no examination determined their qualifications. These licenses simply authorized the midwife to baptize infants in an emergency since so many babies died at birth and bad roads often made impossible the services of a minister.

"At the beginning of the eighteenth century," says Harvey

Graham, "an increasing number of people began to take the view that midwives should have rather more instruction than was implied by the usual Bishop's license. At that time any woman could practice midwifery if recommended by a few matrons, took a formal oath and paid a fee of 18s 4d. There was no more attempt at examination than there had been in the seventeenth century but the oath was more elaborate. The would-be midwife had to forswear child substitution, abortion, sorcery and overcharging, all of which practices were common. The Bishop's license was no guarantee of skill, and women tended to take up midwifery because they needed money and had no experience of anything else. Women who were widowed or very old became midwives 'as if a woman were more expert in that art for her dotage.' " [2]

As time went on, more and more male "midwives" or, we would say, doctors, were called in to assist in difficult cases and often seemed to get better results than the women. In London, the Chamberlens, four generations of them, were distinguished practitioners of obstetrics. Peter Chamberlen the Elder was physician to King James I and his Queen Anne in 1612. There was great mystery about what was called the Chamberlen "secret." When the great doctor arrived for a delivery he always brought with him a large wooden box decorated with gilded carvings. This was taken with him to the patient's room, and no one but a Chamberlen was admitted. Years later one of the Chamberlen wives found the famous box hidden in the attic under a trap door. When she opened the box the "secret" was revealed: a pair of forceps! Hugh Chamberlen of the fourth generation of these doctors delivered Princess Anne (later Queen Anne) of a baby who soon died, as did the rest of her seventeen children. Since Hugh had no heir, the story of the "secret" leaked out, and by 1708, forceps were in general use.

The medical profession of Susanna's day was far from competent. There were then four categories of doctors: the physician, the surgeon, the apothecary, and the unlicensed practitioner. The training of all of them was inadequate. Matthew Wesley, the brother of Samuel, practiced in London as "a civilian, doctor of physic and a chirugeon," but he seems to have had little formal preparation for his chosen profession beyond visits to various spas in Europe. John Wesley himself later wrote a book on "Primitive Physic"—a medical curiosity to this day.

The religious life of England was at a low ebb in these times. True, there were godly ministers in that day and parsonages that belonged in the same category with that of the Wesleys. Bishops Butler and Berkeley were spoken of as almost saintly, but "taken as a class, the clergy of the eighteenth century were gross and unspiritual because they represented a faith exhausted of all spiritual force." [3] The historian Green quotes Bishop Burnet as branding the English clergy of his day as "the most lifeless in Europe." [4]

Speaking of the beginning of the 1700's, William Fitchett says: "A new century was dawning but it seemed as if in the spiritual sky of England the very light of Christianity was being turned by some strange and evil force into darkness." [5] And if the true test of any age and the most optimistic is the picture of its religion, then England's portrait at that time was a dour and sinister one.

Gone were the days of the heroism of such men as the parents and grandparents of Susanna and Samuel Wesley. Then English clergymen were persecuted for their stand on religious freedom and were not afraid to lose all for conscience' sake. Now it had come about that for the most part even the leaders of the Anglican Church fawned upon their lordly patrons and winked at the excesses of the Court. Or else, they lived it out in their influential parishes, going through the stodgy performance of their duties with none of the urgency that belongs to those with a divine calling.

As for the ordinary rural clergy, Lord Macaulay gives us this unhappy picture of them:

The coarse and ignorant squire, who thought that it belonged to his dignity to have grace said every day at his table by an ecclesiastic in full canonicals, found means to reconcile dignity with economy. A young Levite—such was the phrase then in use—might be had for his board, a small garrett, and ten pounds a year, and might not only perform his own professional functions, might not only be the most patient of butts and of listeners, might not only be always ready in fine weather for bowls, and in rainy weather for shovel-board, but might also save the expense of a gardener or of a groom. Sometimes the reverend man nailed up the apricots, and sometimes he curried the coach-horses. He cast up the farrier's bills. He walked ten miles with a message or a parcel. If he was permitted to dine with the family, he was expected to content himself with the plainest fare. He might fill himself with the corned beef and the carrots; but, as soon as the tarts and cheese-cakes made their appearance, he quitted his seat, and stood aloof till he was summoned to return thanks for the repast, from a great part of which he had been excluded.

Perhaps after some years of service he was presented to a living sufficient to support him; but he often found it necessary to purchase his preferment by a species of simony, which furnished an inexhaustible subject of pleasantry to three or four generations of scoffers. . . . A waiting-woman was generally considered as the most suitable helpmate for a parson. . . .

In general, the divine who quitted his chaplainship for a benefice and a wife found that he had only exchanged one class of vexations for another. Not one living in fifty enabled the incumbent to bring up a family comfortably. As children multiplied and grew, the household of the priest became more and more beggarly. Holes appeared more and more plainly in the thatch of his parsonage and in his single cassock. Often it was only by toiling on his glebe, by feeding swine, and by loading dungcarts, that he could obtain daily bread; nor did his utmost exertions always prevent the bailiffs from taking his concordance and his ink-stand in execution. It was a white day on which he was admitted into the kitchen of a great house, and regaled by the servants with cold meat and ale. His children were brought up like the children of the neighboring peasantry. His boys followed the plow, and his girls went out to service. Study he found impossible, for the advowson of his living would hardly have sold for a sum sufficient to purchase a good theological library; and he might be considered as unusually lucky if he had ten or twelve dog-eared volumes among the pots and pans on his shelves.[6]

Again quoting Green: "Of the prominent statesmen of the time the greater part were unbelievers in any form of Christianity and distinguished for the grossness and immorality of their lives. . . . The rural peasantry . . . were left without much moral or religious training of any sort. 'We saw but one Bible in the parish of Cheddar,' said Hannah More at a far later time, 'and that was used to prop a flower pot.' " [7]

The truth is, the dissolute reign of Charles II had left a dark mark upon English life which was not quickly erased, and even the Church was affected by it. Religion had been wrung dry of the compelling power that should have been its life blood. Deism had come to full flower during this period. God was not denied, but he had created the universe, given it its laws, and then gone off to some far distant spot where he had no touch with mortals. Religion was governed by reason and cold logic, and anything bordering on enthusiasm was anathema. Worship was observing the stated forms traditionally laid down; most sermons were dry homilies that furnished no spiritual manna for the living of one's days. Many Englishmen felt a postive scorn of religion. Others filled the family pew because it was traditional to do so, but their routine worship was troubled by no pangs of conscience regarding their less privileged countrymen.

It was for such a time as this that John Wesley, reared in a dismal swamp in Lincolnshire by parents of pious heritage and strong religious faith, was called to arouse all England from its spiritual lethargy.

THE EPWORTH RECTORY REBUILT AFTER THE
FIRE . . . THIS TIME WITH SUBSTANTIAL BRICK.

4
LIFE
at EPWORTH

By the time Susanna was ensconced in the Epworth parsonage she had been married about eight years. Samuel received his Bachelor of Arts degree at Oxford in June, 1688, was ordained deacon in the Church of England seven weeks later, and was given a London curacy which paid him twenty-eight pounds a year. It was several years later that he received his Master of Arts degree from Cambridge. In February, 1689, he was ordained priest and given an appointment as chaplain on a man-of-war with the munificent salary of seventy pounds a year and plenty of time to devote to his beloved writing.

But he and Susanna were deeply in love, so he resigned the chaplaincy after a few months and they were married. They settled down to a London curacy which paid a meager thirty pounds. Their lodgings in Holborn were decidedly forlorn, but their hopes were high. From early Oxford days Samuel had earned many a guinea from his poems and other articles. Now he was beginning to come into his own as a writer.

About this time, in 1690, John Dunton started the publication of a penny paper called the *Athenian Gazette*. This paper, published three times a week, was a question-and-answer periodical designed to cover the whole area of literature. Associated with him were Samuel Wesley whose field was religion and philosophy, and Richard Sault for mathematics. The *Gazette* won high praise from the leading literary and political figures of the day who eagerly submitted articles for publication.

The three contributors to the *Athenian Gazette* also produced an amazing publication called *The Young Student's Library*. One of the most important "pieces" in this work was written by Samuel Wesley, then only thirty years old. It bore the pretentious title, *A Discourse concerning the Antiquity, Divine Original and Authority of the Points, Vowels and Accents that are placed in the Hebrew Bible*. This heavily named treatise received high praise from some of the leading scholars of the day for its extensive study of Hebrew and Oriental languages and vast knowledge of Rabbinical writings. Incidentally, there was no gratuity for this scholarly production.

Events moved swiftly for the young Wesleys. Their first child Samuel was born at Holborn—a difficult birth for Susanna—and when the baby was but four months old they moved to South Ormsby, Lincolnshire.

The living there was obtained largely through the influence

of the Marquis of Normanby whose country seat was located in South Ormsby. Samuel served as the great man's chaplain and ministered to the villagers as well, but there was ample time also for his literary pursuits. The *Gazette* folded in 1696, unfortunately for it had given promise of being lucrative.

During the South Ormsby pastorate Samuel published a long poem entitled: *The Life of our Blessed Lord and Saviour Jesus Christ*. This he dedicated, after the custom of the day, to Queen Mary. Perhaps, too, he hoped by this act to win preferment with Her Majesty, head of the Church of England.

Like the rest of his poetry, this work was of dubious literary merit. Certainly his output in this field was copious and was worthwhile to him financially, but his devoted son John could never rate his poems any higher than fair. He wrote too hastily and with little revision, and too long—much too long. Of his erudition, however, there can be no doubt. This is evidenced by his many writings and by the high esteem in which he was held by the scholars of his time.

Life at South Ormsby gave Susanna little time to indulge her nostalgic longings for the London of her girlhood. Her first daughter, Susanna, arrived the first year of their stay in this parish, to live only a few months. Next came Emilia, followed in short order by twins, Annesley and Jedediah who soon took their place beside little Susanna in the churchyard. Susanna gave birth to another daughter named Susanna, with Mary's advent the next year—seven children in seven years!

Things were always happening to the fiery, forthright rector Samuel Wesley, and this was true during his pastorate at South Ormsby. The dissolute life at the Hall, as the Marquis' home was called, was constantly galling to Samuel, a strict disciplinarian where morals were concerned. To add to his embarrassment, the mistress of Lord Castleton, then renting the Hall, had several times called upon Mrs. Wesley at the Rectory. Things reached a climax one afternoon when, upon returning home, Samuel found this undesirable visitor seated cozily at his fireside with Susanna. With little ado he "took her by the hand and very fairly handed her out."

From then on the handwriting was on the wall for Samuel in South Ormsby. He retained both the friendship and the chaplaincy of the Marquis, indeed that gentleman recommended Samuel for an Irish bishopric, but now the rector was *persona non grata* in that parish.

How Mr. Wesley came by the Epworth living is not known. He thought Queen Mary had suggested it before her death two years prior to his appointment. Be that as it may, he assumed the duties of his new parish called St. Andrew with a complete dedication which never diminished during his long and chequered career in that rural milieu so unsuited to his talents and temperament. Susanna must have been aware of the tragedy of this assignment, for in later years she wrote her brother in India:

"And did I not know that Almighty Wisdom hath views and ends, in fixing the bounds of our habitation, which are out of our ken, I should think it a thousand pities that a man of his brightness, and rare endowments of learning and useful knowledge, in relation to the church of God, should be confined to an obscure corner of the country, where his talents are buried, and he determined to a way of life for which he is not so well suited as I could wish . . . ."

From the very outset at Epworth the impossibility of their financial circumstances was frighteningly apparent to both Susanna and Samuel, so that Samuel with high but unfounded hopes perforce turned to farming on their glebe lands, for economic salvation. Poor Samuel! Energetic and industrious he certainly was, but fundamentally the rector was a city man and a scholar and totally incapable of learning the ways of a farmer. His parishioners, of course, could have helped him, but he seemed unable to make proper rapport with these country folk and they only stood by, ridiculing his awkwardness. When his barn fell down during their first year at Epworth, added expense was needed to replace it.

In his business affairs Samuel proved equally inept, so that Susanna with her customary poise took over the management of the glebe lands and the finances. She was careful, however, to do nothing that would discredit her husband. She was ever loyal and firmly taught her children to be so.

There were few idle moments for Susanna. Mehetabel, or Hetty, arrived during the first year at Epworth, followed in rapid succession by five other babies, all of whom died. Baby Anne put in her appearance in 1702. The "churching of Susanna," one authority observed, referring to the Prayer Book's office for "The Thanksgiving of Women after Childbirth," was "an annual affair at Epworth." That period of English history knew nothing of planned parenthood: Susanna lost nine of her nineteen children before they reached maturity. All this with only one servant most of her married life!

John Wesley in later life speaks of the serenity with which his mother transacted business, wrote letters, and conversed, surrounded by her thirteen children. This means that three of the nine lived beyond early infancy. But the life-span of these three was not very long, and they do not figure in any histories of the Wesley children.

In spite of all their adversities and the ever complicating spectre of poverty, the rectory of the Wesleys was a happy home,—"they had the common fame of being the most loving family in the county of Lincoln," writes Adam Clarke.

The Wesley children were "a cluster of bright, vehement, argumentative boys and girls, living by a clean and high code, and on the plainest fare; but drilled to soft tones, to pretty formal courtesies; with learning as an ideal, duty as an atmosphere, and fear of God as law." [1]

Life at Epworth could not be called completely idyllic, however, for Susanna and Samuel differed often. Indeed, later in life, she wrote to her son John indicating her worry that she and his father "rarely agreed on a particular matter." Theirs was the union of two very strong characters. Samuel's quick-tempered pronouncements were met by the calm, well-reasoned opinions of Susanna, who on her side had difficulty in changing once she had made up her mind. But there was mutual respect as well as love between these two people. Susanna attests her feeling for her husband by her famous letter to her brother Samuel Annesley in India, who had entrusted some business transactions to Samuel with dire results. "He is not fit for worldly business," she admitted with characteristic truthfulness but added with undying devotion: "Where he lives, I will live, and where he dies, I will die and there will I be buried. God do so unto me and more also if aught but death part him and me."

As for Samuel, no one could deny his love for Susanna after reading these lines which are a part of his *Life of Christ,* written early in his married life:

> She graced my humble roof, and blest my life,
> Blest me by a far greater name than wife;
> Yet still I bore an undisputed sway,
> Nor was't her task, but pleasure, to obey;
> Scarce thought, much less could act, what I denied,
> In our low house there was no room for pride;
> Nor need I e'er direct what still was right,
> She studied my convenience and delight.
> Nor did I for her care ungrateful prove,
> But only used my power to show my love.
> Whate'er she asked I gave, without reproach or grudge,
> For still she reason asked, and I was judge;
> All my commands, requests at her fair hands,
> And her requests to me were all commands.[2]

Some writers have too greatly belittled Samuel Wesley and given him a low rating in comparison with his unusual wife. He has been accused of shrewd conniving for preferment,

even of setting fire to the Epworth rectory on the occasion of
its burning, not to mention the accusation of an utter lack of
understanding for his daughters. But regarding his daughters
we must remember that he, too, should be judged according
to the standards of his own day. Perhaps there were things
about Susanna that irked him; he was full of a spontaneous
wit, and not even Susanna's most ardent admirers have ever
attributed much of a sense of humor to her. Perhaps it was a
trial to Samuel also that Susanna would not always follow the
accustomed submissive pattern of a wife of the eighteenth
century.

These are mere matters of conjecture. What we do know
is that the Epworth parsonage produced children of exceptional
qualities whose love and concern for one another persisted to
the end of their lives.

There must have been some relief from oppressive debts
during their early stay at Epworth, for there is a letter
written by Samuel in December of 1700, to the Archbishop of
York, relating at length his pecuniary difficulties. This appeal
resulted in the needed help.

The Wesleys settled down to the life of their parish. Susanna
was content to let Samuel pursue what he considered to be in
line with his duties—his writings, his trips to London—but
she remained at home. Her entire life was centered about the
rearing of the children, attention to the business of the home,
and the life of the parish. She had few congenial friends in
Epworth and is said to have made only one trip to London in
the forty years of her sojourn at Epworth. But she was never
bored.

Samuel took an active part in the wider affairs of the
Established Church. Early in his pastorate at Epworth he was
selected to preach the sermon at the time of the bishop's
visitation in the neighboring town of Gainsborough; three
times he was sent to the Convocation in London, as the

representative of his diocese. Each trip meant a personal expense of fifty pounds. The family finances could ill afford this outlay, but it was the Lord's work, and the budget had to be stretched to meet it.

Samuel Wesley was a Tory through and through and his belief in the divine right of kings remained firm as ever when William of Orange and his queen supplanted the Stuarts in 1688. But Susanna, who was a Jacobite, considered the Prince of Orange to be a usurper. When one evening at family prayers she failed to say "Amen" to the rector's prayer for the king, he took her to task for it. She stated her views in no uncertain sound, and, as John Wesley's *Journal* relates the story, she was "inflexible." "Sukey, if that be the case," rejoined the rector, "we must part, for if we have two Kings, we must have two beds." He thereupon took his departure for London in high dudgeon and did not return until Anne's accession to the throne saved face for him.

An interesting sidelight on this episode is contained in an excerpt from a letter of Mrs. Wesley to her confidante, Lady Yarborough of Snaith Hall, in which Susanna states that she had told her husband that "since I'm willing to let him quietly enjoy his opinions, he ought not to deprive me of my little liberty of conscience." [3]

It is true that a trip to the Convocation coincided in time with this departure, but the episode exemplifies how uncompromising they both were in what they considered matters of conscience. It was following their reconciliation that John, their most famous son, was conceived and born.

From the very beginning things never went very smoothly in the local parish. Samuel Wesley was a strict disciplinarian where his parishioners were concerned. He minced no words in his preaching, and tact was never one of his virtues. On one occasion he came upon a parishioner cutting ears of corn from the tithe sheaves and putting them in his own sack. Samuel took the man bodily to the marketplace of the village, emptied the bag before the dumbfounded people, related the story of the thievery, then stalked home to the rectory.[4] He also forced some of his wayward flock to stand barefoot on the cold church floor Sunday after Sunday in penance for some misdemeanor.

The people of that area were disturbed anyhow. When Samuel came to Epworth they were still in the throes of settling the terms under which their island home had been drained by the Dutch engineer Vermuyden, brought there for that purpose. In return for his services Vermuyden was to receive a third of the land, the Crown another third, and the natives were to get the remaining third. Working out this triple ownership entailed a complicated and bitter controversy. Vermuyden brought in workmen from his own country who proved unwelcome to the native people. Then Vermuyden sold part of his holdings and retained a part. To add to the general confusion, some of the local inhabitants were loath to relinquish their rights. There was much double and crooked dealing in the whole affair, making the people of Epworth more rebellious and violent than even their natural bent called for. Accordingly, they expressed their frustration by violent acts—burnings, tearing down dykes, and the like.

All in all, the early days at Epworth were a time of misfortune for the Wesleys. During a dry spell sparks caught in the thatched roof of the rectory and two thirds of the house was destroyed. No one was hurt and the books and library were left intact, but rebuilding was costly. To add to the Wesleys' troubles, the parishioners hated their rector's High Church ways and his fierce royalist sympathies. He had once written a letter to a fellow minister condemning the Dissenters' educational system, and without his knowledge the letter was published. This did not increase his popularity, particularly when he was indebted to the Dissenters for his early education. Furthermore, his flock bitterly resented their rector's censure of their morals, and took it out on him and his family in many ways. They burned his flax crop, taunted the Wesley children, pried the hinges off the rectory doors. They stabbed his cows so that they gave no milk and once even tried to cut off the legs of the house dog.

Things came to a climax in the local elections of 1705. With great zeal but insufficient knowledge Wesley promised his vote to the wrong candidates; then, discovering his mistake, publicly repudiated his commitments. This infuriated the men of Epworth. His life was threatened, and while he was away casting his vote the townspeople kept up an all-night harassment of Mrs. Wesley and the children, drumming, shouting, and firing pistols directly under the window where Susanna lay, weak from the recent birth of a baby. The baby was being cared for across the street by a nurse who, exhausted after the night's disturbances, slept so heavily that she rolled on the baby and smothered it. When the nurse awoke and discovered what she had done, she became almost distracted, rushed into the rectory, and threw the baby into the arms of the servant. The maid ran to Mrs. Wesley's room and, before Susanna was half awake, placed the dead baby into her arms. "She composed herself as well as she could," says her husband, "and that day got it buried."

The election fiasco did not end here for the Wesleys. One of the enraged parishioners, to get even with Samuel, demanded the immediate payment of a debt of the rector's, amounting to a mere thirty pounds. Samuel did not have the ready cash, but his creditor would not give him even one day of grace, had him arrested and forthwith carried off to the debtors' prison at Lincoln Castle.

Susanna was left at home with all the care of the family and only ten shillings with which to feed them. Three of the cows she depended on for food for the children had dried up, due to the stabbings they had received. But her great concern was for her husband who had "little above ten shillings" in his pocket and must provide food for himself in the jail. Susanna sent him her rings—all she had—but gallant Samuel returned them to her. Samuel, in turn, frustrated over leaving his "poor lambs in the midst of so many wolves," again sought the help of the Archbishop for his desperate family, and again the appeal was not in vain.

Archbishop Sharpe decided to pay a personal visit to Epworth to see for himself how the mistress of the parsonage was faring. It is easy to imagine the flutter of excitement that ran through the household as the great prelate with his entourage appeared at the door. But Mrs. Wesley was not in the least perturbed. After all, she had grown up in the company of some of the leading divines of England; why should she be awed by a mere archbishop? There is no doubt as to the impression this visit made upon the kindhearted cleric, as he witnessed the indomitable courage of the proud lady of that parsonage, her intelligence and dedication in surroundings that bespoke extreme poverty.

After promising her relief from their present distress and the payment of her husband's debts, the archbishop said to Susanna:

"Tell me, Mrs. Wesley, whether you ever really wanted bread?"

"My Lord," was her candid reply, "I will freely own to your Grace that, strictly speaking, I never did want bread. But then, I had so much care to get it before it was eat, and to pay for it after, as has often made it very unpleasant to me. And I think to have bread on such terms is the next degree of wretchedness to having none at all."

The archbishop is said to have left a generous gift of money on the table as he departed. Mrs. Wesley, gracious lady that she was, quietly accepted it in the spirit in which it was given.

Meanwhile Samuel took up life in the Lincoln prison with the optimism of a Micawber. Confident that Susanna would carry on at home with her customary inventiveness and efficiency, he tackled the self-appointed task of rector to his fellow jailbirds.

"Now I am at rest," he wrote to the archbishop, "for I am come to the haven where I've long expected to be," adding that perhaps he might "do more [good] in this new parish than in my old one." [5] He preached to the prisoners on Sunday, had morning and evening prayers, and, with the help of the Society for Propagating Christian Knowledge, was able to distribute Christian literature to his fellow inmates. Again Archbishop Sharpe, backed by others of the clergy, came to Samuel's rescue. They arranged for the payment of his debts, and after three months in the Castle he was released to return to his family at Epworth.

Never once did it occur to Samuel to seek another parish, in spite of advice to the contrary. "'Tis like a coward to desert my post because the enemy fire thick upon me," was his rejoinder.

In 1704, at the age of fourteen, Susanna's eldest son Sammy, as he was affectionately called, went off to Westminster to school. This must have been a painful separation for Mrs. Wesley. Though she was rigidly impartial in the treatment of her children, if she had a favorite it was probably young Samuel. This may be accounted for by the fact of his difficult birth and the awful anxiety under which she lived until he was five years old. For it was not until this age that he spoke his first words. Then, too, Samuel was the oldest child, and she always leaned on him. Indeed, as long as he lived he was a tower of strength to his family and took upon himself more than his share of their cares and financial woes.

Samuel went about his work as faithfully as ever after his return from prison. In the fall of 1706, Patty was born, and in December of the following year, Charles. Samuel was as faithful as ever in his ministrations as pastor of his flock, visiting them from house to house, but he was not popular.

Had the writer of the Book of Job lived at a later period he might well have had the Wesleys in mind when he penned his famous proverb: "Man is born unto trouble, as the sparks fly upward." This was literally true of the rectory family on the night of February 9, 1709, when the sparks not only flew upward but flew in all directions, and fire completely destroyed the house. Some authorities, including John Wesley himself, believed the fire to have been of incendiary origin—the fenmen had been guilty of similar depredations before. However, this is hardly a fair accusation. A thatched house of lathes and plaster, candles for light, plus the rector's absentmindedness, may easily have added up to a fire.

The story of the fire, pieced together from accounts written by both Susanna and Samuel, is a dramatic one. Susanna, who was within a short time of what proved to be her last *accouchement,* had retired for the night; so had the rest of the family. Hetty who occupied a little room up under the eaves, was awakened by fire falling on her bed. She gave the alarm which was taken up by passersby on the street. Samuel was aroused by the cry of "fire" from outside and with but little on besides his nightshirt led the way downstairs, the two older girls arousing the rest of the children. Susanna would have tarried to bring out the little money they had upstairs, but Samuel bade her "fly for her life." When they reached the front door he remembered he had left the door key upstairs. So holding his breeches over his head he dashed back to recover it, the stairs by that time being already ablaze. No one had time to put on any clothes.

With the opening of the street door the northeast wind drove in the flames, making all return to the upper floor impossible. Meanwhile some of the children had gotten out through the windows, the rest through a door into the garden. Susanna was in no condition to climb out the window nor could she get to the garden door. Finally, she waded through the flames at the front door and collapsed outside in the garden. The maid, aroused by Susanna, brought out the baby in her arms, telling John and the other children sleeping with her in the nursery to follow.

By this time the fire had reached such proportions that all was in the wildest confusion. No one knew whether other members of the family had escaped until Samuel finally could assemble his little brood about him in the garden—all safe except John whose cries could be heard from the upper floor. Several times Samuel tried to mount the stairs to fetch him out, but the whole stairway was ablaze. Thinking the boy lost, Samuel fell on his knees in the yard and commended his soul to God. Apparently the little fellow had not awakened at the maid's call. When he did and tried to go through the door the flames prevented him. But the crowd outside caught a glimpse of the tiny figure at the window, for he had climbed up on a chest beside it.

"Fetch a ladder!" shouted one man—but there was no time for that. Then a big practical villager ("who liked me," Samuel later narrated) braced himself against the wall while a smaller man climbed up on his shoulders. The first time the slighter man fell; the second try was successful, and strong arms lifted the little fellow out of the window. It was in the nick of time, for just then the whole roof fell in.

"Come, neighbors," cried Samuel, as the Wesley family shivered beside the charred ruins of their home, "let us kneel down; let us give thanks to God . . . ; let the house go. I am rich enough."

Yes, Susanna and Samuel were abundantly wealthy in the courage and fortitude necessary to rise above calamity, but this catastrophe robbed them of every material thing they owned: their home, their furnishings, the books, Dr. Annesley's precious papers, and their own writings.

Ever afterward John Wesley referred to himself as "the brand plucked from the burning." Perhaps his miraculous escape deepened in him a sense of his calling. Certainly Susanna believed he was saved for some great purpose, for she later wrote: "I do intend to be more particularly careful of the soul of this child, that Thou has so mercifully provided for."

Kezziah, the youngest child, was born in March, 1709, a matter of weeks after the ordeal of the fire.

To Mrs. Wesley's great distress, following the fire the family had to be separated until the rectory could be rebuilt. Emilia, then seventeen years old, cared for her mother for nearly a year in lodgings at Epworth. Young Susanna and Hetty were sent to London to live with their uncle, Dr. Matthew Wesley; young Susanna stayed with Samuel Annesley until his departure for India. John is said to have stayed in the home of a minister. The rest were scattered about in the homes of the villagers of Epworth. During this dispersion the children learned rough ways and uncouth speech quite foreign to their upbringing in the rectory, and it took time and great patience on the part of their mother, when they finally got back home, to correct such things.

Samuel, with the help of the Ecclesiastical Commissioners, succeeded in rebuilding the rectory, this time with substantial brick. The family, however, never completely recovered from the loss incident to the fire. Years later Susanna wrote to her brother in India: "Mr. Wesley rebuilt his house in less than one year; but nearly thirteen years are elapsed since it was burned, yet it is not half furnished, nor his wife and children half clothed to this day."

THE CHILDREN WERE PUT INTO A
REGULAR METHOD OF LIVING.

5

SUSANNA as MOTHER and TEACHER

In the England of Susanna's day elementary education, where there was any, was often in the hands of a tutor. Sammy was the only one of Mrs. Wesley's children to receive such instruction. He was enrolled at Mr. John Holland's private school in Epworth, but this gentleman was so eccentric and imbibed to such excess that Samuel was removed from his school at the end of a year. Besides, in the destitute Wesley family there were no funds for schooling, so Susanna permanently took over the education of her children.

At the proper time the three boys were sent to preparatory schools, Samuel and Charles to Westminster, John to Charter-house; the girls had no other education than that received at home, with the exception of Susanna and Hetty during their stay in London following the fire.

The wonder is that any one person could have maintained such a schedule as Susanna Wesley set for herself. In addition to her constant childbearing, the conduct of her household with insufficient domestic help, her management of the tithes and glebe lands, and her parish duties, she kept school for many years for her large family and did it well.

To accomplish such a gargantuan task, she had to work out a systematic method of procedure. The statement by Fitchett that the childhood piety of John Wesley was "constructed on the principle of a railroad time table" is therefore not surprising.

Historians are unanimous in saying that Susanna was a born teacher. She had the patience for it. On one occasion her husband, sitting in on a session of the school, counted the number of times she repeated one bit of information to the same child. Always impatient, he could sit quietly no longer. "I wonder at your patience," he cried. "You have told that child twenty times the same thing."

"If I had satisfied myself by mentioning it only nineteen times," was the calm reply, "I should have lost all my labor. It was the twentieth time that crowned it."

Years later one of Charles Wesley's sons was to say of his grandmother: "She had the happy talent of imbuing a child's mind with every kind of useful knowledge in such a way as to stamp it indelibly on the memory." More important than that, Susanna Wesley gave to her pupils a love of learning that was to flower out, particularly with her brilliant sons, in an astonishing way.

We are indebted to John Wesley for the account, in her own words, of his mother's method for educating and training her children. From earliest childhood John had always insisted on knowing the reason behind everything that happened. Indeed, his persistent "why's" almost irritated his father, though he also admired that quality in his son. "I protest, sweetheart," said father Samuel to Susanna. "I think our Jack would not attend to the most pressing necessities of nature unless he could give reason for it." True to his nature, John sought to find out everything about his mother's method of education which she had evidently worked out for herself. After several requests his mother finally yielded to his entreaties.

The end of a letter dated February 21, 1732, furnishes one of the rare expressions of Susanna's inner feelings:

The writing anything about my way of education I am much averse to. It cannot, I think, be of service to anyone to know how I, who have lived such a retired life for so many years, used to employ my time and care in bringing up my children. No one can, without renouncing the world, in the most literal sense, observe my method; and there are few, if any, that would entirely devote above twenty years of the prime of life in hopes to save the souls of their children, which they think may be saved without so much ado; for that was my principal intention, however unskillfully and unsuccessfully managed.

Then follows her plan of education, set down in a subsequent letter to John, dated July 24, 1732:

According to your desire, I have collected the principal rules I observed in educating my family.

The children were always put into a regular method of living, in such things as they were capable of, from their birth; as in dressing and undressing, changing their linen, etc. The first quarter commonly passed in sleep. After that they were, if possible, laid into their cradle awake, and rocked to sleep, and so they were kept rocking till it was time for them to awake. This was done to bring them to a regular course of sleeping, which at first was three hours in the morning, and three in the afternoon; afterwards two hours till they needed none at all. When turned a year old (and some before) they were taught to fear the rod and to cry softly, by which means they escaped abundance of correction which they might otherwise have had, and that most odious noise of the crying of children was rarely heard in the house, but the family usually lived in as much quietness as if there had not been a child among them.

As soon as they were grown pretty strong they were confined to three meals a day. At dinner their little table and chairs were set by ours, where they could be overlooked; and they were suffered to eat and drink (small beer) as much as they would, but not to call for anything. If they wanted aught they used to whisper to the maid that attended them, who came and spake to me; and as soon as they could handle a knife and fork they were set to our table. They were never suffered to choose their meat, but always made to eat such things as were provided for the family. Mornings they always had spoon meat; sometimes at nights. But whatever they had, they were never permitted at those meals to eat of more than one thing, and of that sparingly enough. Drinking or eating between meals was never allowed, unless in case of sickness, which seldom happened. Nor were they suffered to go into the kitchen to ask anything of the servants when they were at meat: if it was known they did so, they were certainly beat, and the servants severely reprimanded.

At six as soon as family prayer was over, they had their supper; at seven the maid washed them, and, beginning at the youngest, she undressed and got them all to bed by eight, at which time she left them in their several rooms awake, for there was no such thing allowed of in our house as sitting by a child till it fell asleep.

They were so constantly used to eat and drink what was given them that when any of them was ill there was no difficulty in making them take the most unpleasant medicine; for they durst not refuse it, though some of them would presently throw it up. This I mention to show that a person may be taught to take anything, though it be never so much against his stomach.

In order to form the minds of children, the first thing to be done is to conquer their will and bring them to an obedient temper. To inform the understanding is a work of time, and must with children proceed by slow degrees, as they are able to bear it; but the subjecting the will is a thing which must be done at once, and the sooner the better, for by neglecting timely correction they will contract a stubbornness and obstinacy which are hardly ever after conquered, and never without using such severity as would be as painful to me as to the child. In the esteem of the world they pass for kind and indulgent whom I call cruel parents, who permit their children to get habits which they know must be afterwards broken. Nay, some are so stupidly fond as in sport to teach their children to do things which in a while after they have severely beaten them for doing. When a child is corrected it must be conquered, and this will be no hard matter to do, if it be not grown headstrong by too much indulgence. And when the will of a child is totally subdued, and it is brought to revere and stand in awe of the parents, then a great many childish follies and inadvertences may be passed by. Some should be overlooked and taken no notice of, and others mildly reproved; but no wilful transgression ought ever to be forgiven children without chastisement less or more, as the nature and circumstances of the case may require. I insist on the conquering of the will of children betimes, because this is the only strong and rational foundation of a religious education, without which both precept and example will be ineffectual. But when this is thoroughly done, then a child is capable of being governed by the reason and piety of its parents, till its own understanding comes to maturity, and the principles of religion have taken root in the mind.

I cannot yet dismiss the subject. As self-will is the root of all sin and misery, so whatever cherishes this in children ensures their after wretchedness and irreligion: whatever checks and mortifies it, promotes their future happiness and piety. This is still more evident if we farther consider that religion is nothing else than doing the will of God and not our own; that the one grand impediment to our temporal and eternal happiness being this self-will, no indulgence of it can be trivial, no denial unprofitable. Heaven or hell depends on this alone, so that the parent who studies to subdue it in his child works together with God in the renewing and saving a soul. The parent who indulges it does the Devil's work; makes religion impracticable, salvation unattainable, and does all that in him lies to damn his child body and soul for ever.

Our children were taught as soon as they could speak the Lord's prayer, which they were made to say at rising and bedtime constantly, to which, as they grew bigger, were added a short prayer for their parents, and some collects, a short catechism, and some portion of Scripture as their memories could bear. They were very early made to distinguish the Sabbath from other days, before they could well speak or go. They were as soon taught to be still at family prayers, and to ask a blessing immediately after, which they used to do by signs, before they could kneel or speak.

They were quickly made to understand they might have nothing they cried for, and instructed to speak handsomely for what they wanted. They were not suffered to ask even the lowest servant for aught without saying "Pray give me such a thing"; and the servant was chid if she ever let them omit that word.

Taking God's name in vain, cursing and swearing, profanity, obscenity, rude ill-bred names, were never heard among them; nor were they ever permitted to call each other by their proper names without the addition of brother or sister.

There was no such thing as loud playing or talking allowed of, but everyone was kept close to business for the six hours of school. And it is almost incredible what may be taught a child in a quarter of a year by a vigorous application, if it have but a tolerable capacity and good health. Kezzy excepted, all could read better in that time than the most of women can do as long as they live. Rising out of their places, or going out of the room, was not permitted except for good cause; and running into the yard, garden, or street, without leave, was always esteemed a capital offence.

For some years we went on very well. Never were children in better order. Never were children better disposed to piety, or in more subjection to their parents, till that fatal dispersion of them after the fire into several families. In these they were left at full liberty to converse with servants, which before they had

always been restrained from, and to run abroad to play with any
children, bad or good. They soon learned to neglect a strict observ-
ance of the Sabbath, and got knowledge of several songs and bad
things which before they had no notion of. That civil behaviour
which made them admired when they were at home, by all who
saw them, was in a great measure lost, and a clownish accent and
many rude ways were learnt which were not reformed without
some difficulty.

When the house was rebuilt, and the children all brought home,
we entered on a strict reform; and then was begun the system
of singing psalms at beginning and leaving school, morning and
evening. Then also that of a general retirement at five o'clock
was entered upon, when the eldest took the youngest that could
speak, and the second the next, to whom they read the psalms for
the day and a chapter in the New Testament; as in the morning
they were directed to read the psalms and a chapter in the Old
Testament, after which they went to their private prayers, before
they got their breakfast or came into the family.

There were several bye-laws observed among us. I mention
them here because I think them useful.

1. It had been observed that cowardice and fear of punishment
often lead children into lying till they get a custom of it which
they cannot leave. To prevent this, a law was made that whoever
was charged with a fault of which they were guilty, if they would
ingenuously confess it and promise to amend should not be beaten.
This rule prevented a great deal of lying, and would have done
more if one in the family would have observed it. But he could not
be prevailed upon, and therefore was often imposed on by false
colours and equivocations which none would have used but one,
had they been kindly dealt with; and some in spite of all would
always speak truth plainly.

2. That no sinful action, as lying, pilfering at church or on the
Lord's day, disobedience, quarrelling, etc. should ever pass un-
punished. . . .[1]

3. That no child should be ever chid or beat twice for the same
fault, and that if they amended they should never be upbraided
with it afterwards.

4. That every signal act of obedience, especially when it crossed

upon their own inclinations, should be always commended, and frequently rewarded according to the merits of the case.

5. That if ever any child performed an act of obedience, or did anything with an intention to please, though the performance was not well, yet the obedience and intention should be kindly accepted, and the child with sweetness directed how to do better for the future.

6. That propriety [the rights of property] be invariably preserved, and none suffered to invade the property of another in the smallest matter, though it were but of the value of a farthing or a pin, which they might not take from the owner without, much less against, his consent. This rule can never be too much inculcated on the minds of children; and from the want of parents or governors doing it as they ought, proceeds that shameful neglect of justice which we may observe in the world.

7. That promises be strictly observed; and a gift once bestowed, and so the right passed away from the donor, be not resumed, but left to the disposal of him to whom it was given, unless it were conditional, and the condition of the obligation not performed.

8. That no girl be taught to work till she can read very well; and that she be kept to her work with the same application and for the same time that she was held to in reading. This rule also is much to be observed, for the putting children to learn sewing before they can read perfectly is the very reason why so few women can read fit to be heard, and never to be well understood.[2]

Mrs. Wesley's practice which she termed "conquering their will," or "subjecting the will" merits a word of comment. At first glance one might think this meant breaking the spirit of her children, but nothing could be further from the truth.

To manage such a large family, attend to the farming, and conduct school daily for all her children Mrs. Wesley was obliged to work out a rigid regimen. She set up her household under as strict a discipline as that of a company of soldiers, each child being amenable to properly constituted authority which was hers. Like the military, Susanna's stringent regime was not simply for more efficient handling of a large group of people, but as better preparation of each member of the company for the battle of life ahead. Her system was always geared to a future when each individual child should have reached a state of maturity and could regulate his own life. The formation of character was ever the end of all her striving.

In evaluating Mrs. Wesley's methods which now seem so hard and inflexible, we must remember that hers was a hard age, an age of harshness to children. The cruel floggings by tyrannical schoolmasters, as pictured by Dickens and other writers of a later period, were not exaggerated. Susanna's discipline was mild in comparison. "Strength guided by kindness," ruled in the Wesley household, and the love Susanna bore each individual child is evidenced by the fact that for many years she set aside a special time every week for each child. In a letter to his mother, John refers in tender terms to his Thursday evenings spent with her, wishing they could be continued.

Nowhere is there any record of resentment on the part of the Wesley children against their mother's method of education. In fact, John tried to carry out her plan to the letter in his Kingswood School.

It may well be that the modern child psychiatrist will read but the first paragraph of Mrs. Wesley's rules and then superciliously toss them aside. Certainly her system appears strangely outmoded in an age when the child's freedom to express itself is so dominant in educational thinking. As to the "rod," its very presence is horrifying to many who set the pace for rearing twentieth-century children.

But "crying softly at one year of age" may not be an impossible achievement. Experts on babies' reactions now pride themselves on being able to classify their cries according to the stimulus that evokes them—hunger, anger, etc. Perhaps these cries can be regulated by correcting the condition involved! And there are those who, from a distant childhood, can still hear the echo of a gentle mother's tones, when tensions mounted in the nursery: "Children, keep your voices down! Children, keep your voices down!" Strangely enough, the admonition was usually effective.

In spite of the fact that Mrs. Wesley's system of education runs counter to the tenets of modern child guidance experts, it is worthy of study not only for historic interest but because her method worked. The children she reared developed into members of one of the most eminent families in English history, remarkable for their looks, their intellect, and their sterling character. Her daughters, though limited by their environment and the time in which they lived, were spirited and well educated. There was nothing craven about them. As for her three distinguished sons, the eminence they attained in their several spheres would never have been possible had they been "crushed" in spirit.

There is sound common sense and good child psychology in some of Mrs. Wesley's rules, particularly the "bye-laws," as she called them. The marvel is that she could carry them out with such precision, with due regard for the individual temperaments of all her children. It must be remembered, too, that the state of the Wesley exchequer permitted the purchase of few textbooks, and Susanna taught her children with what material she found on the library shelves, chiefly the Bible, and what she wrote herself.

But all the credit for the Wesley children's education does not belong to Susanna. Quite evidently, Samuel played an important role in this also. Susanna was no classicist, but her husband was acknowledged to be "one of the best classical scholars of his day," and it was he who took care of this part of his children's schooling. It is highly probable that his sons began their study of Greek and Latin under their father before they went off to preparatory school.

Of course, there were no institutions of higher learning for women in the time of the Wesley girls, but if there had been,

Susanna and Samuel could never have afforded college for seven daughters. It was with almost superhuman effort and great sacrifice that they managed to send the boys through Oxford, and to an Englishman the training of his boys was vastly more important than that of the girls. The education of the Wesley daughters was, however, by no means neglected, even to instruction in Latin and Greek. Hetty, one of the brightest of the girls, is said to have read Greek at the age of eight and later wrote for *The Gentleman's Magazine*. Martha in later life was a favorite of the great Dr. Samuel Johnson and held her own among the literary figures who frequented his house.

What sort of play the young Wesleys engaged in is known only sketchily. Susanna had no patience with such worldly amusements as ball room dances. She did not send her children to dancing school but is said to have had a dancing master come to the house for lessons. She did play cards and other games with her children at home.

We have no knowledge of what sort of toys were played with in the Epworth rectory; perhaps they were handmade by local craftsmen. We do know that the children had plenty of room on their own premises for wholesome fun, and like most English children of that period, they had the whole countryside to roam over.

The education of Susanna's children was not finished when they left home. Both their father and mother followed them wherever they were, with letters of wise counsel. The children for their part held their parents in deep affection, and love dominated this family circle to the very end. Long after he had become a famous man, John Wesley expressed his deep yearning to see Epworth again. "Epworth," he wrote in a letter dated June 26, 1784, "which I still love beyond most places in the world."

6
OLD JEFFREY
the GHOST

A ghost in the rational and orderly household of the Wesleys sounds preposterous, but a ghost they had, and a well authenticated ghost at that.

This unexpected visitor first arrived at the Epworth rectory in early December, 1716—John was thirteen then—and for a number of weeks thereafter he kept the house very lively with mysterious noises—groanings and loud knockings from all parts of their abode. There was the sound of breaking bottles

at the foot of the stairs, chains rattling, the noise as of a carpen-
ter planing, or a jack being wound. Sometimes the house shook
from top to bottom. One night when the din made sleep impossible, the rector and his wife decided to investigate, and
hand in hand descended the stairs. When they reached the hall
below, according to Susanna's account, "a large pot of money
seemed to be poured out at my waist, to run jingling down
my nightgown to my feet." ("Have you dug in the place where
the money seemed poured at your feet?" wrote Samuel, Jr.
who was always involved in the family's finances.) As Mr.
Wesley and Susanna proceeded into the kitchen that night,
their mastiff came whining to them and wedged himself between them, cowering in fear. They searched every room in
the house and saw nothing unusual, but the "rattle and thunder" continued for more than an hour throughout the rectory.

The ghost actually showed himself on only four occasions
and in varying forms: Susanna saw him under a bed as a
headless badger; Robin Brown, the manservant, caught a
glimpse of the same figure near the kitchen fireplace, and at
another time a creature like a small rabbit came out from
behind the dining room fireplace beside Robin, turned swiftly
around five times and disappeared. To Sukey and Hetty the
apparition resembled a man in a long, trailing nightgown. He
made himself heard, however, at any time he took a notion,
day or night.

This was no kindly spirit, this "Old Jeffrey," as Emilia
playfully named him. He rather fitted the poltergeist definition
—a noisy imp who harassed the entire family with his devilish
tricks.

Jeffrey had his favorites, too. The door latches would be
lifted by a mysterious hand to let the girls pass through. Susanna, always practical, expressed the wish that she be not disturbed from five to six during her private devotions, and,
oddly enough, the wish was granted.

The Wesley ghost had its strong political likes and dislikes and was quite evidently an ardent follower of the Stuarts, for it always kept up a frightful din overhead when Mr. Wesley prayed for King George and the Prince at family prayers. This interruption made the little rector so angry that he would defiantly say the prayer over again and always with the same result. On the other hand, Old Jeffrey was mischievous at times. John Wesley, in his account, tells of a "gentle tapping" at the head of the girls' beds between nine and ten at night. They then usually said to one another: "Jeffrey is coming, it is time to sleep."

During the ghost era, Samuel, Jr. was teaching at Westminster, John was at Charterhouse, and Charles was newly registered as a student at Westminster, so the boys had little first-hand knowledge of the strange happenings at home. Young Samuel, alarmed by the extent of Jeffrey's performances, demanded a letter from each member of the family giving his or her individual account of the phenomena, and for once the correspondence from Epworth took on a personal character. The usual letters from Susanna and Samuel to their children were impersonal, dealing solemnly with great events or principles of conduct and the like, with few of the personal touches which would be priceless to historians of this family. Old Jeffrey, if he did nothing else, upset this cool detachment. During the period of his visitation the letters from various members of the family, and especially the rector's diary, reveal reactions so characteristic of their writers as to be amusing.

Susanna, logical and unbiased, discredited the reports of her children and the servants until she could thoroughly evaluate the antics of the ghost for herself. Even then she first attributed the noises to rats until, after fruitlessly sounding a horn throughout the house to run them off, she became firmly convinced that no human creature or animal was capable of making such disturbances. In a letter to her son Samuel, weary of his persistent questionings regarding the ghost, she wrote (March 27, 1717):

"I cannot imagine how you should be so curious about our unwelcome guest. For my part, I am quite tired with hearing or speaking of it: but if you come among us, you will find enough to satisfy all your scruples, and perhaps may hear or see it yourself."

The dauntless little rector defied Old Jeffrey whose politics he resented anyhow: "Thou deaf and dumb devil," he cried in a loud voice, "why dost thou frighten the children that cannot answer thee? Come to me in my study that am a man." The ghost immediately simulated Samuel's knock (the particular knock he always used at his own gate and door) "as if it would shiver the boards in pieces," says Tyerman, "and away it went." [1]

After that it constantly annoyed Mr. Wesley in his study which had hitherto been spared its visitations. Samuel on one occasion even got out his pistol after the ghost, but one of his friends of the clergy, Mr. Hoole, who was with him at the time, convinced him that one cannot shoot a spirit.

At first the children trembled in sheer terror at the mysterious noises, even in their sleep; but Old Jeffrey's comings became so frequent that they got accustomed to the intruder and accepted him as a member of the family. They found they could tease and anger him by making personal remarks about him, and this turned into a sport with them. To little Kezzy, Old Jeffrey became a favorite playmate. She chased his tappings from room to room, gleefully stamping on the floor with her tiny feet and hearing the answering knock in return.

Nancy reported that the ghost walked behind her as she swept the room, seeming to repeat the sweeping after her. On one occasion the bed on which she was sitting was lifted several times. This performance was in the presence of several others in the family.

Mr. Hoole, the neighboring clergyman, was asked to spend the night at the rectory during the height of Jeffrey's disturbances, to "conjure" the ghost. He wrote his account to Samuel,

Jr.; Robin Brown wrote his version, and so did Betty Massy, the maid.

Hetty seemed to be the one most troubled by the ghost. Its frequent knockings on her bed made her turn and twist in her sleep. It followed her more often than the others, too. Emily reported to her brother Samuel that the ghost knocked repeatedly under Hetty's feet, "and when she had removed, it has followed, and still kept just under her feet, which was enough to terrify a stouter person." [2] Susanna wrote to Sammy that "it commonly was nearer her [Hetty] than the rest, which she took notice of; and was much frightened, because she thought it had a particular spite at her. I could multiply particular instances, but I forbear." [3]

Why did she "forbear"? One of the greatest mysteries about the affair of the Wesley ghost is the absence of any recorded account by Hetty. Young Susanna in a letter to her brother Samuel (March 27, 1717) says: "I should farther satisfy you concerning the disturbances; but it is needless, because my sisters Emilia and Hetty write so particularly about it."

But where are Hetty's letters? Were they lost or purposely concealed by her brothers? In all the carefully assembled data on Old Jeffrey there is no record of Hetty's own impressions, nor is there any excuse made for their omission. Could Hetty have been the unconscious intermediary in all these impish goings-on at the rectory, since she was the person most disturbed by it all? We shall probably never know but must add these to the other mysteries related to this case.

Every possible attempt was made to connect the antics of the ghost with some individual or individuals. They could not have been traceable to any member of the Wesley family or to the servants, because all were affected by its visits not only separately but in groups. Outsiders could not be blamed either—Old Jeffrey's presence was manifested too often and in too varied ways. More and more it became an accepted fact that no natural explanation could be found for the ghost but that he had to belong to the realm of the extra-natural.

Susanna tried to interpret the visits of the ghost as a foreboding of disaster or death—some accident to one of the boys or the death of her brother in India. This explanation fortunately proved groundless. John for a time believed that Old Jeffrey was sent to pester his father because the rector left his family after Susanna failed to say *Amen* to the prayer for King William. Emilia gives her opinion about the ghost in a letter to her brother Samuel, undated but said to have been written about February 11, 1716-17:

"I am so far from being superstitious, that I was too much inclined to infidelity; so that I heartily rejoice at having such an opportunity of convincing myself, past doubt or scruple, of the existence of some beings besides those we see."

By the end of January, 1717, the annoyances of Old Jeffrey had about come to an end, though Tyerman reports that they were repeated at long intervals to the end of March of that year, then ceased altogether. Long after—thirty-four years after, to be exact—Emilia writes in a letter to her brother John, dated February 16, 1750: "You won't laugh at me for being superstitious if I tell you how certainly that *something* calls on me against any extraordinary new affliction; but so little is known of the invisible world, that I, at least, am not able to judge whether it be a friendly or an evil spirit."

As a postscript it may be reported that long after the Wesleys had gone and over a hundred years after the first visit of the ghost, he is said to have returned to Epworth rectory and so harassed the occupants of the house that they went to London to be rid of him.

Of all similar disturbances of this sort, the Epworth poltergeist is undoubtedly one of the best documented—the rector's diary, the entire correspondence with Samuel, Jr., preserved in his own handwriting, John's account set down years later and published in the *Arminian Magazine* when he was an old man—all this makes out a strong case. One must bear in mind also that the Wesleys who were subjected to this strange visitation were sensible people. For them "no fairies still danced in the woods," nor were they superstitious like the simpler folk of the Lincolnshire parish. Credence must therefore be given to their narratives about the ghost. It is no wonder, then, that leading scientists and authorities in the field of the occult have made the Epworth ghost the subject of extensive research.

It would be inappropriate here to recount at length their findings. Some conclusions were absurdly impossible, others worthy of some consideration; but no one to this day has unraveled the mystery of Old Jeffrey. The Wesleys all linked him with the supernatural; Luke Tyerman, their historian, shared their opinion; so did Robert Southey, the deist. In his *Life of* [John] *Wesley,* Southey writes: "It would be end sufficient if sometimes one of those unhappy persons who, looking through the dim glass of infidelity, see nothing beyond this life, should, from the well-established truth of one such story, be led to a conclusion that there are more things in heaven and earth than are dreamt of in their philosophy."

Susanna characterized the happening in her utilitarian way: "If they [such apparitions] could instruct us how to avoid any danger, or put us in the way of being wiser or better—there would be sense in it, but to appear to no end that we know of unless to frighten people almost out of their wits, seems altogether unreasonable." Sammy's summation was epigrammatic: "Wit, I fancy, might find many interpretations, but wisdom none." The rector, true to form: "It would make a glorious penny book for Jack Dunton."

The whole episode of the ghost made a profound impression upon John Wesley. As a boy of seventeen, he who always needed a reason for everything amassed all the facts regarding Old Jeffrey, and as time went on he carefully evaluated them. No one, even in the age of reason in which John Wesley lived, could have weighed every detail of this strange happening with colder logic and more impartial judgment than the Founder of Methodism, and his decision was in favor of the supernatural. Here was a queer phenomenon, perfectly documented, that could not be explained away, and this fact made an indelible impression upon him. Andrew Lang of a later day, an authority on the study of ghosts, says Old Jeffrey "made a thoroughfare for the supernatural" through John Wesley's brain.

Through his long lifetime there was ever for John Wesley a consciousness of good as well as evil forces in the realm of the spirit. It was his firm belief in the reality of an unseen world and its implications for man when this earthly sojourn ceases that helped to make Wesley the compelling leader he was.

Old Jeffrey was still in his mind when, at the age of sixty-six years and with the perspective of almost a lifetime, he published, in his Methodist *Arminian Magazine,* his own factual account of this mysterious visitation of his childhood.

SUSANNA'S KITCHEN SERVICES: SOME FAMILIES
WHO SELDOM WENT TO CHURCH NOW WENT CONSTANTLY.

7

SUSANNA
in the PARISH

If only the Wesleys could have known how famous they were
to become, they might have kept a journal, or at least a diary,
to give to posterity an account of the "Wesley dispersion"
while the rectory was being rebuilt after the fire.

Did Mrs. Wesley keep school in the lodgings she occupied
till the new house could be made ready, or was she not able
to keep school at all? What kind of time did young Susanna
and Hetty have in London during this period? Their sojourn

in the big city must have been an exciting change from the restricted life of the remote flats of the "Isle of Axholme." Dr. Matthew Wesley, brother of Samuel, took them into his home; but did they visit also uncle Timothy Wesley and Mrs. Dyer, the sister of father Samuel, and grandmother Wesley, all of whom apparently lived in London? Part of the time young Susanna stayed with her uncle Samuel Annesley, before he went to India. Did he inherit the fine qualities of his famous father, the Reverend Samuel Annesley? Unfortunately, this period in the life of these two Wesley daughters is a frustrating blank. Mr. Annesley, incidentally, promised young Susanna financial help, but in one of Mrs. Wesley's letters we are told that this was never forthcoming.

Kezziah, the youngest Wesley child, was doubtless born in the lodgings where Susanna took refuge after the fire. She was named for one of the daughters of Job, probably by her father who lived and breathed in the atmosphere of that Old Testament patriarch. Kezzy, as she was commonly called, was delicate from the first, and constant attention must have been lavished upon her by both Mrs. Wesley and faithful Emilia, who cared for her mother during this trying interlude.

Susanna redeemed the time during the rebuilding by rewriting her Manual or treatise which had been destroyed in the fire. The purpose of this Manual was the religious instruction of the older children, and in it she set forth a detailed explanation of the "evidences of revealed religion." The new writing reproduced the old and added a treatise on the chief articles of the Christian faith based upon the Apostles' Creed. She addressed it to Sukey in London, on January 13, 1709/10, but it was intended for the instruction of the other children as well. Dr. Adam Clarke holds that this work was entirely original with Mrs. Wesley, and, though some of her conclusions may not be acceptable to a twentieth-century theologian, it is a remarkable production from a woman of Susanna's day. It was during the interval after the fire that she composed also her dissertation on the Ten Commandments.

The fire wreaked even more disastrous havoc upon Samuel's scholarly writings. He had, with great expenditure of time and labor, made alterations in his *Life of Christ*. This together with all his other writings was destroyed. The only product of Mr. Wesley's pen that remained untouched by the flames was his beautiful hymn, "Behold the Savior of Mankind," a priceless Methodist heritage which to this day holds an honored place in the Methodist Hymnal.

Before the fire Samuel Wesley had already begun work on the most pretentious writing of his career: *The Dissertations on the Book of Job*. This was to occupy most of his spare time for the remaining years of his life. The volume comprised fifty-three dissertations, written in Latin, with Hebrew and Greek quotations. He had carefully read the Book of Job in Hebrew and in the Septuagint, had collated the versions and added notes. Then he had secured Walton's Polyglot Bible which contained the original texts of both the Old and New Testaments in Hebrew and Greek, with all the ancient versions then known. These he also collated with his first work, adding more notes. All this meticulous work was destroyed by the fire, every page of it, and his precious Polyglot Bible as well.

This was a mighty blow, but Samuel Wesley's spirit was as indomitable as that of his wife. With thankfulness in their hearts for the deliverance of their family they set to work *de novo*. Samuel procured another Polyglot and, in addition to his previous work, consulted all the commentators he could find, even making the trip to the library of Lord Milton at Wentworth House, accompanied by his son John. Here he was accorded every courtesy, and Mr. John Wesley was asked to preach in the parish church on the Sunday morning of their stay.

All the papers and records of Susanna's father, the Reverend Samuel Annesley, were also destroyed in the fire.

The new rectory was about a year in construction, and this time it was of sturdy brick, in Queen Anne style, a most creditable building still in use today.

Rebuilding caused no curtailment of parish duties. Though the rector was never popular—his lack of tact and the strictness of his discipline toward his parishioners prevented that—he was a conscientious pastor to his flock. He knew them all by name and regularly visited them from house to house. These visits were not merely social but were pastoral in nature, with inquiries into the conduct of the children and the spiritual state of each household.

Susanna's participation in the work of the parish during the early years of their stay in Epworth receives no comment by historians. Doubtless her time was more than filled with child bearing and the management of rectory and glebe. But not too long after the family's return to the newly built rectory she assumed a startling role in the life of St. Andrew's parish. It happened this way:

Samuel Wesley not merely pursued his regular duties and scholarly writing, but his fellow clerics considered him also quite a leader in the wider work of the Established Church. Three times they chose him to represent his diocese at the Convocation in London.[1]

One of these notoriously long meetings began in 1710. Though there was no expense account to draw upon and the Wesley exchequer was in its usual state of depletion, Samuel arranged for a curate, Mr. Inman, to manage the affairs of the parish in his absence, and set out for London. Susanna remained at home to care for the family as best she could with the meager resources at her command.

Soon after Mr. Wesley's departure, Emilia found in her father's study the story of the Danish mission to Tranquebar. Emilia read it aloud to her mother. The exploits of these Danes were most inspiring to Susanna. She felt that, in comparison, her own life was not as worthwhile as it might be and decided to do something about it in the only place possible for her—her own home. "I thought I might live in a more exemplary manner in some things," wrote Susanna to Samuel in London. "I might pray more for the people, and speak with more warmth to those with whom I have an opportunity of conversing." Could it be that Susanna bore her share of guilt for the lack of rapport with the people of Epworth?

It was under the inspiration of this book that Mrs. Wesley decided she should give more time to each of her children individually, so she set up a schedule of conferences at the only time available, in the evenings, and continued this practice as long as her children remained under the rectory roof.

The Reverend Mr. Inman proved a poor substitute for Samuel. In the curate's sermon on Sunday mornings (the only service he conducted) he continually harped on one theme: the obligation to pay one's debts. Since it was common knowledge in the parish that the rector was usually in arrears, the sermons were considered to be aimed at Samuel himself. Susanna bore the humiliation with composure.

During her husband's long absence there was no afternoon service at the church, and she felt obligated to have evening worship for her family. These services were held in her kitchen and consisted of the singing of psalms and the reading of prayers and a short sermon selected from her husband's library shelves. First the servants begged to come, then some of their relatives and friends, and finally the neighbors, so that the attendance increased to more than two hundred, with some unable to gain admittance. How one kitchen could contain such a congregation is difficult to understand, but these are Susanna's figures, and she was never inaccurate.

Dutifully Mrs. Wesley sent a report of her kitchen meetings to her husband in London. Nor was hers the only report. Mr. Inman was infuriated because Susanna had a larger attendance at her little service than he had on Sunday morning. He protested to the rector against his wife's evening "conventicle," as he called it, and had several of his friends join him in the protest. Samuel's reply was not long in coming, and it was anything but favorable.

His objections which were expressed at length can best be summarized by giving the gist of Susanna's answer to them:

"As to its looking particular [unseemly], I grant that it does; but so does almost everything that is serious, or that may anyway advance the glory of God or the salvation of souls, if it be performed out of a pulpit, or in the way of common conversation."

In answer to her husband's contention that it was unsuitable for a woman to conduct such a meeting, she wrote:

"As I am a woman, so I am also mistress of a large family. And though the superior charge of the souls contained in it lies upon you, as head of the family, and as their minister; yet in your absence I cannot but look upon every soul you leave under my care as a talent committed to me." Later in the letter, being very much a woman of the eighteenth century, she expresses herself as dissatisfied with presenting the prayers of the people to God because of her sex: "Last Sunday I fain would have dismissed them before prayers, but they begged so earnestly to stay, that I durst not deny them."

"As for your proposal of letting some other person read," she further wrote, "Alas! you do not consider what a people these are. I do not think one man among them could read a sermon, without spelling a good part of it; and how would that edify the rest? Nor has any of our family a voice strong enough to be heard by such a number of people."

In a later letter to her husband, Susanna describes the good effects of these meetings: "Our meeting has wonderfully conciliated the minds of this people toward us, so that we now live in the greatest amity imaginable. . . . Some families who seldom went to church, now go constantly; and one person, who had not been there for seven years, is now prevailed upon to go with the rest."

And then comes her final paragraph which not only demonstrates the force of Susanna Wesley's personality, but also how politic she was:

"If you do, after all, think fit to dissolve this assembly, do not tell me that you desire me to do it, for that will not satisfy my conscience; but send me your positive command, in such full and express terms as may absolve me from all guilt and punishment, for neglecting this opportunity of doing good, when you and I shall appear before the great and awful tribunal of our LORD JESUS CHRIST."

Susanna won out! How could it be otherwise? When the rector returned to his parish, the kitchen services were discontinued in favor of evening worship at the church, but the old spirit of suspicion and animosity toward the rector was forever gone.

John Wesley, in his account of this unusual happening, says that his mother, "as well as her father and grandfather, her husband, and her three sons, had been in her measure and degree a preacher of righteousness."

Interestingly enough, Susanna spoke of her kitchen congregation as "our Society," and actually these meetings were conducted in much the same way as the Methodist Societies later formed by her son. Perhaps this whole episode is another reason for the title fittingly given to Susanna Wesley: "The Mother of Methodism."

There was a streak of stubbornness in Samuel Wesley, and to satisfy himself as to his curate's competence as a preacher he invited Mr. Inman to preach in the sanctuary and assigned him this text: "Without faith it is impossible to please God." The topic seemed safe enough, but the curate forthwith adapted it to a fifteen-minute homily on the obligation to pay one's debts! The rector was convinced.

The period of Samuel Wesley's attendance upon the Convocation of 1711, as it was called, was an eventful one for the family back home. Beside the kitchen meeting episode, five of the children, including John, had smallpox during their father's absence. Susanna must have excelled as a nurse as well as a teacher, for there is nowhere any mention of disfiguring aftereffects of this dread disease upon the Wesley children.

Whether Samuel brought back from London some monetary gifts from friends and patrons to help him with his debts, as he did when he returned from his first trip to Convocation in 1701, is not known. His biographers do not mention such a windfall.

Samuel, Jr. had been away from home for several years by this time, and the second break in the family life at Epworth came in 1714 when John, not yet eleven years old, went off to Charterhouse School in London. Sammy was by that time teaching at Westminster. It was a great comfort to Susanna and Samuel that John could be near his older brother, and the devoted parents kept in close touch with both sons by frequent letters. There was never any need to urge the boys to study —their love for learning had been fostered at home almost from their infancy. Susanna's letters were confined mostly to matters of conduct and devotions, while Samuel's never omitted instruction about their health. "Run around the garden three times each morning," was father Samuel's advice to John, and good advice it was.

Charterhouse had a fine tradition, but it was severe and hard. Under the prevailing fag system the smaller boys ate what was left on the plates after the stronger lads had helped themselves to what they wanted. Here discipline was strict and unyielding. After six years of such rigorous education, John Wesley left Charterhouse a hardier character with a tougher body. This training was to stand him in good stead for the demanding life that was to follow. It is recorded that at the age of eighty-five, John Wesley walked six miles to an engagement. The rigor of the vast program he mapped out for himself is well known.

One of the firmest beliefs of both Susanna and Samuel

Wesley was in the divine right of kings. To a person of the twentieth century such a doctrine sounds ridiculous, but it was widespread in Mrs. Wesley's time and accounts for some of the positions taken by both Susanna and her husband.

In her "Occasional Papers," written about 1705, Susanna expresses her view on this subject: "I cannot tell how to think that a King of England can ever be accountable to his subjects for any mal-administration or abuse of power. But as he derives his power from God, so to Him only he must answer for his using it." Four years earlier when Susanna and Samuel had their famous tiff over the prayer for William and Mary at family devotions, her contention was that the current sovereigns were usurpers and therefore the divine right belonged to the Stuarts and the Stuarts alone. She was a staunch Jacobite, as was her son Samuel.

The rector's interpretation of this doctrine had a peculiar twist. During his Oxford days when James II came to the university and demanded in a most dictatorial manner that all its appointees should be Romanists, Samuel is said to have remarked: "I saw he was a tyrant. Though I was not inclined to take an active part against him, I was resolved from that time to give him no kind of support." But not long after this episode, who should write one of the congratulatory poems on the birth of the Prince of Wales (in the book prepared by various representatives of Oxford University) but Samuel Wesley! [2]

In spite of these inconsistencies, the Wesleys were both staunch royalists and trained their children to be so.

Meanwhile life went on as usual at the Epworth parsonage, a miserable life in many respects by twentieth-century standards. In addition to Samuel's three trips to London for Convocation, he apparently made several others to raise money. He had to beg funds for the rebuilding of the rectory, since there was no local parsonage committee in those days to take this off his hands and he did a good job of it. In addition, his own debts at times reached a critical stage, and he had to appeal to friends and patrons to help him out. There was much love in the Wesley household, and lofty thought and a high regard for learning, but comforts were very, very few.

John entered Oxford in 1720, on a Charterhouse fellowship. The accounts of the exploits of the three sons away from home furnished an exciting interlude in the drab life of the rest of the family. At great sacrifice Susanna and Samuel managed to keep the boys in school, but no money was left for the girls. Most of them inherited the good looks of the Annesleys and are said to have had many beaus, but few of the local suitors were of congenial tastes with the Wesley girls. "With minds stored with the music of Homer, and hands working to the pageantry of Milton's verse, they were condemned to be hen-girls and swine-herds on the filth of the water-logged flats of Lincolnshire," was Elsie Harrison's caustic summation of the Wesley daughters' fate.

Emilia, the oldest daughter, bewails the "intolerable want and affliction" of the family, and that they were in "scandalous want of necessities." Her mother was in bed all one winter and even expected to die, while Emilia did her best to keep the large family on a very small sum of money. All the girls told of the scantiness of clothes and funds, and they attributed much of their mother's ill health to lack of "common comforts."

Usually Susanna bore her woes with silent resignation. But in a lengthy epistle written on her birthday to her brother in India and dated January 20, 1721/22, she exposes some of her inner feelings. This is the letter in which she apologizes for Samuel's incompetence in the business affairs entrusted to him by Mr. Annesley. She goes on to say:

What we shall or shall not need hereafter, God only knows; but at present there hardly ever was a greater coincidence of un-prosperous events in one family than is now ours. I am rarely in health. Mr. Wesley declines apace. My dear Emilia, who in my present exigencies would exceedingly comfort me, is compelled to go to service in Lincoln, where she is a teacher in a boarding-school. My second daughter, Sukey, a pretty woman, and worthy a better fate, when, by your last unkind letters, she perceived that all her hopes in you were frustrated, rashly threw away herself upon a man (if a *man* he may be called, who is little inferior to the apostate angels in wickedness) that is not only her plague, but a constant affliction to the family. O sir! O brother! Happy, thrice happy are you, happy is my sister, that buried your children in infancy! secure from temptation, secure from guilt, secure from want and shame, or loss of friends! They are safe beyond the reach of pain or sense of misery: being gone hence, nothing can touch them further. Believe me, sir, it is better to mourn ten children dead than one living; and I have buried many. . . .

The other children, though wanting neither industry nor capacity for business, we cannot put to any, by reason we have neither money nor friends to assist us in doing it. Nor is there a gentle-man's family near us in which we can place them, unless as com-mon servants; and that even yourself would not think them fit for, if you saw them; so that they must stay at home, while they have a home; and how long will that be? Innumerable are other uneasinesses, too tedious to mention; insomuch that, what with my own indisposition, my master's infirmities, the absence of my eldest, the ruin of my second daughter, and the inconceivable distress of all the rest, I have enough to turn a stronger head than mine. And were it not that God supports, and by his omnipotent goodness often totally suspends all sense of worldly things, I could not sustain the weight many days, perhaps hours.[3]

SAMUEL WESLEY . . . WAS BURIED IN THE
EPWORTH CHURCHYARD.

8
EPWORTH
and WROOT

In 1724, Samuel Wesley was given the living at Wroot, in addition to the parish at Epworth. Wroot was four and a half miles from Epworth, its rectory was a dilapidated dwelling with a thatched roof, the parishioners "rustics of the lowest order," and the terrain swampy and uninviting. The living paid fifty pounds a year. The rector's family moved from Epworth to Wroot and occupied the parsonage for several years. Wroot was a desolate place to live in at best, but when the rains were excessive land transportation became impossible. All travel then between the two parishes had to be by boat. There was one partially redeeming feature, however; the family had plenty to eat in the smaller parish. It is possible that the Wesleys rented the Epworth rectory during their sojourn at Wroot. This possibility is substantiated by an excerpt from one of the rector's letters: "I walked sixteen miles yesterday, and this morning, I thank God, I was not a penny worse. The occasion of this booted walk was to hire a room for myself at Epworth, which I think I have now achieved." [1]

Samuel Wesley was jubilant over the prospect of having the two livings instead of one. Emilia was urged to come home, now that there was an increase in the family income. She had had a five-year interval of teaching in a boarding school in Lincoln. It was hard work, but she was able to buy some clothes for herself and had thoroughly enjoyed having money of her own. But the school closed and home, perforce, was the logical place for Emilia.

She had been told, she wrote her brother John, that "this addition to my father, with God's ordinary blessing, would make him a rich man in a few years." Rather tartly she continues:

Then I came home again in an evil hour for me. I was well clothed, and, while I wanted nothing, was easy enough. . . . Thus far we went on tolerably well; but this winter, when my own necessaries began to decay, and my money was most of it spent (I having maintained myself since I came home, but now could do it no longer), I found what a condition I was in: every trifling want was either not supplied, or I had more trouble to procure it than it was worth. I know not when we have had so good a year, both at Wroot and at Epworth, as this year; but, instead of saving anything to clothe my sisters or myself, we are just where we were. A noble crop has almost all gone, beside Epworth living, to pay some part of those infinite debts my father has run into, which are so many, as I have lately found out, that were he to save fifty pounds a year he would not be clear in the world this seven years. So here is a fine prospect indeed of his growing rich! Not but he may be out of debt sooner if he chance to have three or four such years as this has been; but for his getting any matter to leave behind him more than is necessary for my mother's maintenance is what I see no likelihood of at present. . . . Yet in this distress we enjoy many comforts. We have plenty of good meat and drink, fuel, etc., have no duns, nor any of that tormenting care for to provide bread which we had at Epworth. In short, could I lay aside all thought of the future, and could be content without three things, money, liberty, and clothes, I might live very comfortably. While my mother lives I am inclined to stay with her; she is so very good to me, and has so little comfort in the world besides, that I think it barbarous to abandon her. As soon as she is in heaven, or perhaps sooner if I am quite tired out, I have fully fixed on a state of life—a way indeed that my parents may disapprove, but that I do not regard. Bread must be had, and I won't starve to please any or all the friends I have in the world.[2]

Not long after the Wesleys moved to Wroot a newspaper notice announced that Mr. Samuel Annesley was returning to England in one of his company's ships. What an event this was to be for Susanna—a reunion with her long-absent brother and possible financial salvation through his wealth! For such a great occasion Susanna emerged from her retirement and made the journey to London to meet him. This was probably the one visit in forty years which she paid to the city of her birth.

Susanna looked forward in eager anticipation to a happy family reunion. John was to come from Oxford to join his mother in welcoming his homecoming uncle back to England. Then they would all repair to the home of Samuel, Jr. at Westminster to celebrate Mr. Annesley's return. But a bitter disappointment was in store for Susanna. John's finances were in such a state that he could not make the trip to London, and when the East India Company's ship docked, Susanna's brother was not on it, nor was he ever heard from again. There was something very mysterious about Mr. Samuel Annesley's strange disappearance. Repeated inquiries failed to reveal any knowledge of his whereabouts and no trace of him was ever found. His fortune disappeared with him, so that Susanna never received the thousand pounds she had been led to expect from his estate.

Unfortunately, too, the rector's optimism over the financial advantages of the second living were completely unjustified. The fifty pounds which the Wroot living brought in did little more than pay the salary of the curate whom the addition of the second parish made necessary.

During the year 1725, smallpox reached epidemic proportions in Mr. Wesley's parish, and Mrs. Wesley reported to her son John that now every member of their family had had it except herself.

Anne's marriage to John Lambert, a young land surveyor of Epworth, took place early in the family's stay at Wroot. This was one of the few happy marriages for the Wesley girls.

In the spring of 1725 Samuel Wesley had a slight stroke which permanently disabled his right hand. He met this misfortune with an indefatigable spirit. "I have lost the use of one hand in the service," he later wrote to the Reverend Mr. Piggot, Vicar of Doncaster, "yet, I thank God, *non deficit altera,* and I begin to put it [the left hand] to school this day to learn to write, in order to help its lame brother." [3]

As if calamity had not visited the Wroot parsonage often enough, a more serious trouble befell the Wesleys in the fate of Hetty. Late in the spring she left her place of employment at Kelstein to elope with a lover who cruelly betrayed her. She returned home in disgrace. Later that year, in desperation, she made an unsuitable marriage which will be described later on.

Early in the stay at Wroot John wrote his parents, expressing his interest in going into holy orders. His father, in reply,
advised him to take his time in making his decision and
suggested that meanwhile he engage in further study. Thinking of his own work, Mr. Wesley expressed the hope that this
study would be useful to himself in an edition of the Holy Bible
which he was proposing to prepare and continued with a statement that would make helpful reading for ministerial candidates of any age:

"As to the motives [for entering into holy orders] you
take notice of, it is no harm to desire getting into that office,
even with Eli's sons, 'to get a piece of bread'; . . . though a
desire and intention to lead a stricter life, and a belief one
should do so, is a better reason. But this should by all means
be begun before, or else, ten to one, it will deceive us afterwards. . . . But the principal spring and motive, to which all
the former should be secondary, must certainly be the glory of
God, the service of His Church, with the edification of our
neighbour; and woe to him who, with any meaner leading
view, attempts so sacred a work." [4]

Susanna was not in agreement with her husband Samuel
in the matter of John's ordination. "I approve the disposition
of your mind," wrote Mrs. Wesley to John, "and think the
sooner you are a deacon the better; because it may be an
inducement to greater application in the study of practical
divinity, which I humbly conceive is the best study for candidates for orders. Mr. Wesley differs from me, and would
engage you, I believe, in critical learning. . . . I earnestly pray
God to avert that great evil from you of engaging in trifling
studies to the neglect of such as are absolutely necessary.
I dare advise nothing; God Almighty direct and bless you!" [5]

It was his mother's advice that John Wesley followed, and
he was ordained deacon by Bishop Potter, the bishop of
Oxford. The ceremony was delayed for financial reasons but
took place September 19, 1725.

Meanwhile, in the summer of 1725, Samuel Wesley, Jr. with his wife and little son delighted the family at Wroot with a visit. Some historians suggest that this visit was made in an effort to soften the hearts of his parents toward Hetty. However that may be, Samuel, Sr. remained obdurate and unforgiving.

These were eventful years for the Wesleys, the years spent at Wroot. About 1725 when Charles was still at Westminster School, his father received a letter from Garrett Wesley of Donegan Castle, a member of the Irish branch of the family. He inquired as to whether the rector had a son named Charles. Finding that this was so, and having no children of his own, this wealthy relative wished to make Charles his heir. It was an astonishing proposal, but the decision was with finality left to Charles who declined the offer. Susanna never mentioned this incident in any of her letters. Certainly some additional money would have solved many of the Wesley problems, but Charles undoubtedly had good reason for turning down this windfall.

The summer dampness at Wroot caused Susanna much physical discomfort, particularly when heavy rains made the terrain more boggy even than usual. Emilia suffered from malaria in the unhealthy climate and went back to Lincoln in an effort to regain her health and seek employment.

In the midst of the many trials and tribulations of the Epworth Wesleys, one of the happiest events of their lives occurred on March 17, 1726, when John became a Fellow of Lincoln. "Wherever I am, my Jack is Fellow of Lincoln!" was the rector's ecstatic reaction to the news.

Election as Fellow of a college of Oxford was not only an honor but carried with it a yearly stipend, in addition to the regular stipend for whatever academic duties the position required. The Fellows were free to pursue their studies in whatever direction they wished and to do tutoring for additional money. Every Fellow of an Oxford College had the right to a set of rooms in his college, rent free, irrespective of whether he was actually in residence. If he was on leave of absence he was entitled to the rent from his rooms if they were occupied by other members of the College. John Wesley continued as a Fellow of Lincoln for twenty-six years until the day of his marriage.

It had taken no small amount of sacrifice on the part of both Susanna and Samuel to keep John at Oxford, and now had come the fulfillment that made their long-continued efforts worthwhile. This additional income would enable John to support himself and to help with the education of Charles who was just entering Oxford. True, John would require twelve pounds immediately, and the rector was in debt to Sammy for another ten pounds which the latter had loaned to John. This would leave only five pounds with which Susanna must maintain the family until harvest, but the old familiar specter of insolvency paled in the light of this momentous happening in the life of dear Jacky.

Very shortly after his election, John came to Lincolnshire and helped his father through the entire summer. He preached twice each Sunday, either at Wroot or Epworth, visited the people and assisted Samuel with the monumental writing on Job. During this period John began keeping a careful personal diary. This diary was in cipher and is not to be confused with his famous Journal.

John's stay at home was a particular delight to his mother, for he spent many hours with her, reading aloud, and conversing at length about such subjects as theology, his sermons, as well as more personal matters regarding his life and conduct. Here he could also enjoy the company of the Wesley sisters who were then at home. He bought for them many articles they were unable to provide for themselves.

In these maturer years of Susanna, the contemplative side of her nature came more and more to the fore. The years of childbearing were behind her as well as the exacting schedule of her family classroom. She realized that her husband, though as sprightly as ever and making fun of his increasing physical ills, was failing in health. Furthermore, Susanna now knew for a certainty that Samuel would never have another parish, one better suited to his temperament and superior talents. The dreary fenlands of Lincolnshire would be their home to the end of the chapter, with the never ceasing struggle for existence that had characterized their life in this uncongenial parish from the beginning.

Susanna herself was far from well during these years. There were long periods when she was confined to her bedroom and when the girls had to take over her duties in home and glebe. And so, Susanna increasingly turned to her writings, to her letters to the children who had gone out from the home, and to the cultivation of those qualities of life and thought that transcend the material and the earthy.

Years before when Susanna was about thirty years old, with her demanding brood around her, she had adopted the practice of observing an hour of solitary meditation in the early morning—and very early it was—and also in the evening. Later in life she added a noonday period. Nothing was allowed to interfere with this schedule, for she believed that such times of solitary communion were essential if she were to play her exacting role with the composure and self-control it required.

Her thoughts during these hours of private devotion she sometimes wrote down and embodied in letters to her children for their edification. Others of her meditations were later found among her private papers. Here is the beginning of one of her Morning Devotions, undated as were all such writings. It would seem from this excerpt that she is actually addressing herself and exemplifying one of her most striking characteristics: the ability to be almost completely objective in evaluating herself and her growth, or the lack of it, as a personality.

"It is very likely that your humour last night was rather the effect of fancy and passion than of a clear sound judgment. If otherwise, why did you feel uneasiness at another person being out of humour? Was it not pride made you resent contradiction?" [6]

And in a letter to her son John she says: "I heartily wish you would now enter upon a strict examination of yourself." This marked trait of impartial self-analysis which she helped inculcate in her son had decided results in the type of leadership he was able to give in establishing the Methodist movement.

In the early summer of 1727, the rector wrote a number of letters to his sons, John and Charles, which clearly revealed his decline in health. Therefore John prepared to return to Lincolnshire to act as his father's curate for a time.

"I hope I may still be able to serve both my cures this summer," said Mr. Wesley in one of his letters, "or if not, die pleasantly in my last dyke." In another he proposes that John make Wroot his headquarters when he comes, with the rector himself to stay most of the time at Epworth. "The truth is," father Samuel writes, "I am *hipp'd* by my voyage and journey to and from Epworth last Sunday; being lamed with having my breeches too full of water, partly with a downfall from a thunder shower, and partly from the wash over the boat. . . . They tell me I have lost some of my tallow between Wroot and Epworth but that I don't value, as long as I have strength left to perform my office. . . . I am weary, but your loving father."

Still another letter outlines the difficulties of transportation. The Wesley horses had outlived their usefulness, and perhaps John should purchase one on the way there. Excessive rains had washed out some of the crops and made land travel impossible between the two parishes. And running through nearly every letter like a leitmotiv is "Job," with its insatiable calls for help that were never entirely satisfied to Samuel's dying day.

Susanna's physical condition during this period was of great concern to Samuel. One of his letters expresses the wish that both John and Charles come home. Their mother has been seriously ill, he says, and they will find her noticeably altered. Alarmed by this news, they both made the trip to Epworth and happily found their mother greatly improved. While at Epworth they visited Emilia and Kezzy in Lincoln where both were employed at Mrs. Taylor's school. John remained a whole year, acting as curate for his father, then went back to Oxford where, on September 22, 1728, he was ordained a priest in the Church of England. Shortly after this ordination he returned to Epworth to assist his father for another year. He was then recalled to Oxford and at the request of Dr. Morley, the rector of his college, was made moderator of Lincoln.[7]

About this time Mr. Wesley sustained a serious accident. Susanna tells in a letter to John, dated July 21, 1731, how she, Martha, and the maid were riding in the family wagon, with Samuel seated on a chair at the rear of the vehicle. Suddenly, going down hill, the horses broke into a gallop and Samuel was thrown out. Susanna's chair was at the front of the wagon. When the horses quickened their pace, the maid, with great presence of mind, threw her whole weight against Susanna's chair, thus saving her from a fate similar to Mr. Wesley's. Fortunately some neighbors were close by and their quick action and that of the driver saved Samuel's life. He was badly bruised and shaken, but the wheels fortunately had only crushed his sleeve. He was placed in the bottom of the wagon and Susanna held his head between her hands during the slow, painful trip home. The following Sunday he insisted upon conducting his services as usual but did so with noticeable difficulty. Though he continued to go about his duties as if nothing had happened, he was never quite the same after his accident.

By 1731, the Wesleys had returned to the Epworth rectory to live, and it was during this year that Dr. Matthew Wesley, Samuel's brother from London, visited them for the first time.

It was he who had opened his home to young Susanna and Hetty after the fire. Also, he had befriended Hetty during the difficult days following her unfortunate marriage.

Dr. Wesley proved a most agreeable guest, but he was "strangely scandalized," as Susanna put it in a letter to John, "at the poverty of our family," the scant furnishings, and the "mean" clothes the beautiful daughters were forced to wear. He was much impressed by Patty, and during his visit Susanna and Samuel granted his request to permit Patty to go to London to live with him "for a year or two." Actually, she remained a member of his family for a number of years.

Some time after his return to London, Matthew Wesley wrote a scathing letter to his rector brother, censuring him for the poverty-stricken conditions at the Epworth rectory. These he attributed to Samuel's poor management of his salary.

"You have a numerous offspring," wrote Matthew Wesley, "you have had a long time a plentiful estate, and have made no provision for those of your own house, who can have nothing in view at your exit but distress. This I think a black account. . . . I hope Providence has restored you again to give you time to settle this balance." [8]

This letter was in many respects grossly unjust. Samuel Wesley, as anyone acquainted with his circumstances knew, never had a "plentiful estate." Some of the injustice of this letter may possibly be laid to the affluent writer's complete ignorance of the financial demands that were a part of the life of a dedicated parson with a large family, but the letter cut deep. In response, Samuel Wesley wrote at great length to his brother, trying to answer his accusations, or rather, he dictated the greater portion of it to Susanna and to John, since he had by now little use of his hand. This undated epistle is one of the last Samuel Wesley ever wrote. He is proud of his numerous offspring and his rearing of them, he tells his brother. Has he not given to three of them the best education

England affords? He has no doubt of God's provision for his family after his death. As in the families of many English gentlemen, those of his children who are more comfortably off will help the others. He admits his lack of skill in "worldly affairs," but has "all his life labored truly both with his hands, head and heart . . . to get his own living, and that of those who have been dependent on him." (This letter was written in the third person.)

Whether this epistle satisfactorily refuted Dr. Matthew Wesley's charges is not known, but the interchange gave Samuel long thoughts about the future of his family.

This period in Susanna's life was one of bitter dejection. She called it her "sad defection when I was almost without hope." One thinks always of Susanna as mistress of every situation confronting her, an invincible woman. But the infirmities of age were increasing for her, infirmities which seem premature to those familiar with twentieth-century geriatrics. Much of her time she was forced to spend in bed, and there was always the specter of Samuel's failing health and the lack of security for them both in their approaching old age. It is no wonder that from her sickroom, in February 1732, she wrote to John:

"I never did much good in my life in the best health and vigor, and therefore, I think it would be presumptuous in me to hope to be useful now. It is more than I can well do to bear my own infirmities and other sufferings as I ought and would do."

But her actions belied her words. She had ten more years of life ahead of her, and in those years she was to make unprecedented adjustments and help to shape a movement worldwide in its impact.

Samuel's narrow escape from the wagon accident, added to his brother's reproof, made him think more seriously than ever before of what was to become of Susanna should she survive him. Accordingly, he wrote to his son Samuel, proposing to resign the Epworth living in his favor. This would mean that Susanna could continue to live in the rectory and would be tenderly cared for by the oldest son, who had already shared so many of the family's burdens.

But Samuel declined the offer. He knew all too well the inconveniences of Lincolnshire life as compared with London. Besides, he had his own plans about his mother, with no other idea than to provide for her in his own home as long as she lived.

Next, the rector made the same proposal to John, who set down twenty-six reasons why he should not accede to his father's request. Also, he had found out that the chances of effecting a transferal of the Epworth living so as to keep it in the Wesley family were exceedingly slim.

Meanwhile, Susanna and Samuel had taken into their home John Whitelamb, a thin, ungainly youth, a native of Wroot and product of its Charity School. "Poor, starveling Johnny," Susanna called him—a most suitable epithet. John Whitelamb served as amanuensis to the rector in the further compilation of the *Dissertations on the Book of Job*.

John Whitelamb gave promise of becoming a fine scholar. He was an enthusiastic pupil of Mr. Wesley during his stay in the rectory, and poor as they were, the Wesleys managed to send him through Oxford, even clubbing together to supply a gown for him which his own meager resources could not provide. John Wesley was his tutor at the University, serving without pay. After his ordination, John Whitelamb returned to Epworth in the capacity of curate to Mr. Wesley.

Mary Wesley, or Molly, the third of the Wesley daughters, always remained at home. She had a beautiful face but a body shortened and misshapen because of an injury received in infancy, thought to be due to a nurse's carelessness. Molly's nature was as lovely as her face and without a trace of bitterness. She proved very successful in the management of the glebe lands and was her mother's standby, particularly during

Susanna's many spells of illness. She was devoted to her father, too, and more understanding of him than were her sisters.

She and John Whitelamb were, of necessity, closely associated during his years as a member of the Wesley household. After he had finished Oxford and had become Samuel Wesley's curate, he proposed marriage to Mary and she accepted him. The family highly approved of the match, for John and Mary were genuinely in love with each other.

Samuel succeeded in having the living at Wroot transferred to John Whitelamb and promised to supplement by twenty pounds annually the meager fifty pounds which that parish paid. There were few clergymen who were willing to live in such an unattractive place as Wroot, but the Whitelambs loved it and happily began their married life there.

It was short-lived, however. Mary died within a year in childbirth, and baby and mother were buried together in the same grave. Whitelamb quietly served on at Wroot for more than thirty years but lost touch with the Wesleys in after years. He became uncertain in his beliefs, was once almost a deist and at another time leaned toward the Roman faith. However, as the Methodist revival began to spread, Whitelamb had John Wesley preach in his sanctuary—one of the few Church of England pulpits in which Mr. Wesley was then allowed to speak. And when John Wesley preached from his father's grave, September 6, 1742, John Whitelamb was a part of the large audience that heard him. Following this occasion Whitelamb wrote John Wesley a moving letter of appreciation for what the Wesley family, and John particularly, had done for him.

After Mary's death, Whitelamb returned to the Epworth household and was immediately put to work on the *Dissertations on the Book of Job,* as was everyone Samuel could commandeer for the completion of his labor of twenty-five years.

But the end was approaching for Samuel Wesley, and

Susanna knew it. "Your father is in a very bad state of health," she wrote to John; "he sleeps little and eats less. He seems not to have any apprehension of his approaching exit, but I fear he has but a short time to live. It is with much pain and difficulty that he performs Divine Service on the Lord's Day, which sometimes he is obliged to contract very much. Everybody observes his decay but himself, and people really seem much concerned for him and his family."

Meanwhile, Samuel was giving a goodly portion of his ebbing strength to his *Dissertations* which he firmly believed would be so well received that it would bring in a sizable income sufficient to take care of whatever might happen. Poor Samuel! If only he could have been practical enough to put his superior talents to shorter writings of a more popular nature! Many of his contemporaries had done this and had reaped a rich financial harvest thereby. But Samuel Wesley could never lower his sights to a level he considered unworthy of his scholarship.

Adam Clarke says of the *Dissertations:* "It is one of the most complete things of the kind I have ever met with; and must be invaluable to any man who may wish to read this book critically." But the rector's ponderous tome was written entirely in Latin and was doomed from the outset to be a failure as a best seller. The engravings illustrating the book were in general done by John Whitelamb. "Nothing can be conceived more execrable," was one critic's evaluation of them. The frontispiece by Virtue was well done, an engraving of the venerable patriarch, seated in an ancient chair, scepter in hand, dispensing justice. Samuel Wesley must have lived so long with Job's troubles as well as his own that they had become synonymous in his mind, for the face and figure seated in that ancient chair were none other than those of Mr. Wesley himself!

The last trip the rector made to London was in promotion of *Job*. This time his manservant, John Brown, was sent to

London to attend him home. Parenthetically, Samuel Wesley never lived to see the *Dissertations on the Book of Job* in print, but Samuel, Jr. completed the work for him. Six months after his father's death, John Wesley presented the book to queen Caroline to whom it was dedicated. When John Wesley was introduced into the royal presence, relates Adam Clarke, the queen was playing with her maids of honor. She received the volume graciously from John's hand. "It is very prettily bound," she said, and laid it down without once looking at its pages. When John Wesley made his bow and withdrew she returned to her play.

As spring came on in 1735, Susanna knew that her husband's end was near and sent for John and Charles. Mary was dead now, leaving only Kezzy at home to help care for her parents, and John Whitelamb. Emilia came home from Gainsborough where, with a little help from her brothers, she had set up her own school. She and John and Charles took turns in waiting on their father, and he was able to enjoy their company before the end came.

There were dreams unfulfilled for Samuel Wesley as he came to the close of his life: his parish would not pass to his sons but to a man of whom he heartily disapproved; his beloved *Job* was not yet published, and dear Sammy he would not see again in the flesh.

The words of advice he had given his sons from their very infancy continued almost to the last. "The inward witness, son, the inward witness," he repeated to John in those last days, "that is the proof, the strongest proof of Christianity." And to Charles, laying his hand on his youngest son's head: "Be steady. The Christian faith will surely revive in this kingdom; you shall see it, though I shall not."

Susanna was completely "broken down." She went into the sickroom at intervals but each time she fainted and had to be carried out. Death came quietly for Samuel Wesley on

April 25, 1735, at the age of seventy-two, and he was buried in the Epworth churchyard.

John settled up his father's affairs. The debts amounted to little more than one hundred pounds, but when everything was sold and the accounts tallied up there was little left for Susanna. So for the rest of her life she had no choice but to live with her children. Her letters reveal no word of complaint, though there must have been some sorrowful pangs as she left forever the familiar halls of this rectory she had occupied for nearly forty years with her beloved companion.

"But heaven hath a hand in these events," as Shakespeare put it. Susanna Wesley had yet another mission to perform, and she was to perform it well.

THE SEVEN WESLEY DAUGHTERS,
THESE HANDSOME, SPIRITED GIRLS.

9
THE
DAUGHTERS

If Susanna Wesley had sat down at the end of her life and
objectively evaluated it—and she, if anyone, could have been
perfectly impartial in such a summation—she would undoubtedly have concluded that her greatest contribution to the world
was in her children. Upon them she poured out an intelligent
and selfless devotion from the birth of "dear Sammy" to the
last day of her life. No biography of Mrs. Wesley, therefore,

would be complete without a further look into the annals of the ten children she raised to maturity.

In the Epworth family circle life was happy, within the limits placed upon it by its insularity and its relentless poverty. There were frictions at times, as in any family, particularly when its members are as strong-minded as were the Wesleys. But love was always present in this rectory, and however strict the discipline, the children loved and respected their parents and one another.

The young Wesleys were brought up in a Tory and High Church atmosphere, but the Nonconformist background of their parents is also markedly evident in their rearing. "The ethical impulses and the disciplined austerities of the household at Epworth," Dr. Green points out, "testify to a powerful Puritan strain." [1]

History has accorded a prominent place to the sons of Susanna Wesley, and her daughters, naturally, have not figured so largely. It seems strange, though, that extensive research fails to reveal even a single likeness of one of these accomplished girls. They were unusual in their own right, and their story deserves a telling.

For an understandable picture here, it is necessary to have a proper concept of the status of women in eighteenth-century England, to leave the milieu of the twentieth century and make the mental journey into the past when the seven Wesley daughters grew up in the dismal fens of Axholme. This is more than ever essential for a proper understanding of what happened or did not happen to these handsome, spirited girls.

In their day, marriage was about all the future could hold for an English gentlewoman, and failing that, a position as resident governess in a well-to-do-family—a doubtful career at best. *Jane Eyre,* though written after the Wesley era, portrays with eloquent accuracy the predicament in which highbred girls found themselves, a situation which continued until after the Victorian period.

If the English universities had been open to women when the Wesley girls lived—a thought which would have been shocking at that time—Susanna and Samuel would never have managed to finance such schooling for seven daughters. It was hard to scrape together enough to get the boys through and, of course, their education came first. Anyhow, by eighteenth-century standards womanly graces and household know-how were considered to be an English woman's best preparation for life in the home, where it was universally assumed she belonged.

However, there can be no doubt that the Wesley daughters received good educations à la eighteenth century in Susanna's classroom and in Samuel's study, where he instructed his daughters as well as their brothers in higher learning, that is, those of the girls who had the capacity and the desire for it.

But marriage was the great desideratum of English girls, and their parents were equally interested for several reasons. The custom was for parents to turn their attention to making the best matches possible for their daughters. "Since almost everyone regarded it as a grave misfortune to remain single," says the historian George Trevelyan, "women did not count it a universal grievance that their hands should often be disposed of by others. . . . In the upper and middle classes, husbands were often found for girls on the principle of frank barter. 'As to Clokey,' writes her father, Squire Molesworth, 'we shall not have money enough to dispose of her here. So she must be sent to Ireland to seek there a husband at a cheaper rate.'" This quotation is all the more shocking to a modern reader when one realizes that irremediable consequences might result for such a "bartered bride," for divorce was practically unknown during this period. Indeed, in all the twelve years of Queen Anne's reign there were only six English divorces.

The prospect for happiness for Susanna's daughters was never bright. Handsome like all the Annesley women, lively and with all the natural emotions of normal young women,

they were destined for a life of drudgery in isolated surroundings. There must have been young men in and out of
the Epworth parsonage: Emilia in a letter to her brother
Samuel refers to "our lovers." But what lovers! The rough
country lads of the parish were completely unsuitable as life
companions for these cultured girls. True, there were well-
born families in Lincolnshire, but the Wesley daughters had
no proper clothes to appear in such elite society and they never
had the entré there anyway. Certainly the dearth of means of
travel to and from the isolated community in which they lived
limited the range of their acquaintance.

Hetty expressed their plight with striking clarity in a poem
written to her sister Emilia during the latter's stay in the
Wroot parsonage.

> Fortune has fix'd thee in a place
> Debarr'd of Wisdom, Wit and Grace.
> High births and Virtue equally they scorn,
> As asses dull, on dunghills born;
> Impervious as the stones, their heads are found;
> Their rage and hatred steadfast as the ground.
> With these unpolished wights thy youthful days
> Glide slow and dull, and Nature's lamp decays;
> O what a lamp is hid 'midst such a sordid race.

To add to these unalterable disadvantages, their father was
sadly lacking in his understanding of women, their needs or
their sensibilities. Like all English fathers of the eighteenth
century, he was the undisputed "Lord of the Manor" in his
household. Susanna spoke of him as "my Master," and the
children, when writing to him, addressed him as "Honored
Sir." The careers of his sons were his daily concern, but his
daughters were in a different category and always took second
place. No father ever worked more indefatigably for his
family's welfare than did Samuel Wesley, and he loved his
daughters after his impractical fashion, but by our criteria he

was cruel and unfeeling toward them. To be just, though, he too must be judged by the standards of his own time and not by ours.

To Samuel's credit it must be said that in his interference in the love affairs of his daughters—and he did interfere as did their brothers—he was concerned for their future and felt a responsibility in that regard. His callousness and his lack of sympathy for his girls, however, are difficult to understand. There is a rather revealing sentence in a letter written by Samuel Wesley to General Oglethorpe the year before the rector died:

"I thank God I find I creep up hill more than I did formerly, being eased of the weight of four daughters out of seven, as I hope I shall of the fifth in a little longer." [2]

Emilia, the oldest of the Wesley daughters, was the member of the family most critical of her father. She was highly discerning and recognized every fault he had and lashed out against him with great bitterness in her letters to her brothers. She blamed him and his financial irresponsibility for much of the "intolerable want and affliction" of the family. Yet she was withal a dutiful daughter and there was a daughter's love in her too in the context of the "divine right of fathers," the system under which children of that period lived. It was Emilia who came home during her father's last illness and with John and Charles nursed him to the end.

Emilia can certainly be called one of the leading characters in the Epworth drama. She was good-looking and smart, with a measure of tartness thrown in; she had plenty of common sense like her mother and a talent for poetry. As a classical scholar she was a credit to her father's teaching. Her brother John said of her that she was the best reader of Milton he had ever heard.

Emilia was the family standby in many difficult situations. She was a mere girl when she assumed the care of her mother and baby Kezzy following the disastrous fire. It was Emilia

who left her position as governess to nurse her sister Susanna
Ellison through a dangerous illness, and on occasions when
her mother was confined to bed, she frequently took over the
management of the household with very little money at her
disposal.

During a visit to her uncle Matthew Wesley in London, she
met a friend and fellow Oxford student of John Wesley's
named Leybourne, with whom she fell madly in love. The
romance lasted three years but was broken up by a "near
relation," generally conceded to be Samuel, Jr. She later came
to realize that Leybourne was not really in love with her and
would never have made her happy, but the hurt lasted for a
long time.

Emilia early realized that she must provide for herself. She
was twice a governess at Lincoln, the second time at Mrs.
Taylor's boarding school. Here she had the entire supervision
of the school, with long hours and poor pay. Later, with a little
help from John, she set up her own school in Gainsborough
where apparently she was successful.

When she was in her early forties she had another love
affair, this time with a doctor who proved, in her words, "a
faithful friend, a delightful companion and a passionate lover."
This romance was ended also, partly because John objected
to his being a Quaker, and partly because Emilia herself could
not tolerate his intense jealousy and his Whig sympathies. So
she continued her teaching at Gainsborough.

When nearly forty-four years old, and just before her
brother John left for his mission to Georgia in America,
Emilia married an unlicensed apothecary of Epworth named
Robert Harper, long acquainted with the family. John himself
performed the ceremony. Harper was never a financial success
and unfortunately managed to appropriate most of his wife's
earnings. He too was a "violent Whig," she an "unbending
Tory." She is known to have had one child named Tetty. How
long this child lived is not known. Her marriage with Mr.

Harper was short-lived, for he absconded after several years with all of Emilia's savings, leaving her with a sickly infant to nurse and bury.[3]

About five years after her father's death Emilia went to London to live with John. There her brothers took care of her for many years. Her body outlived her memory which had always been prodigious. She died at the age of seventy-nine.

Susanna, the second of the surviving daughters, like Emilia was born at South Ormsby. She, too, was considered beautiful, with a good mind well trained, and a happy nature. During her stay in London after the fire, when she divided her time between her uncles Matthew Wesley and Samuel Annesley, the latter promised to make ample provision for her. When this offer failed to materialize, while she was visiting at Matthew Wesley's home she made a hasty and regrettable marriage without consultation with her parents. The bridegroom was Richard Ellison, a well-to-do gentleman farmer. Although he was from a very fine family he was the very antithesis of young Susanna in his coarseness, vulgarity, and immorality, and in his dictatorial ways. His treatment of his wife was degrading in the extreme and was a constant source of anxiety and mortification to Susanna and Samuel. Samuel called Dick Ellison the "wen of our family"; Susanna was even more severe in her denunciation of her son-in-law, referring to him as "little inferior to the apostate angels in wickedness."

There were four surviving children born of this marriage. A fire later demolished the Ellison home. The family narrowly escaped with their lives, and all of them had to scatter among relatives. After this fire, Susanna Ellison never lived with her husband again, and in order to escape him she hid among her children in London. Ellison made many attempts to win her back but to no avail. On one occasion he had a notice inserted in the newspapers announcing his death, hoping by this means to entice her back to Lincolnshire. She did make the journey there to pay her last respects to the one who had been her husband, only to find him still alive and in good health. She immediately returned to London and nothing could induce her to live with Ellison again.

John, the untiring benefactor of his family, helped her. Indeed, through the years he assisted some of the Ellisons to the third generation.

Richard Ellison gradually lost all his property, went to London, and appealed for help to John Wesley, of all people. John interceded in his behalf with a banker to allow him to benefit from certain charity funds. Mr. Ellison remained in London, but was never able to find Susanna, his wife, and their children, so carefully did they hide themselves from him. Charles Wesley conducted his funeral service and reported that he died in peace. To his wife Sarah, Charles writes: "Sister Macdonald, whom he [Ellison] was always very fond of, prayed with him in his last moments. He told her he was not afraid to die, and believed that God, for Christ's sake, had forgiven him."

The concerned involvement of John and Charles Wesley in the lamentable affairs of the Ellisons is but another example of the family solidarity implicit in the Wesley connection, even toward those who fell far below its standards.

Susanna Wesley Ellison died in December 1764 at the age of sixty-nine.

Mary Wesley, often called Molly, was a baby when Susanna and Samuel moved to Epworth. Her deformed body, often the subject of ridicule by thoughtless passersby, never affected the loveliness of her almost saintly character. Her beautiful face, her gentleness and even temper made her a favorite with all. She was the stay-at-home of the family because of her affliction and accepted the drudgery of the daily round with a sweet spirit. "Patient Grizzle," her brother Charles called her.

There was a particularly close bond of affection between

Molly Wesley and her sister Hetty. At the time of Hetty's great trouble, Molly showed that she had strength as well as gentleness when she stood against the whole family in protest against forcing Hetty into her disastrous marriage.

Mary Wesley never expected romance in her life, but at the age of thirty-eight she found supreme happiness in the ungainly person of John Whitelamb who loved her devotedly in return. The year of married life they had together, doing the work they both loved in the uninviting parish of Wroot, gave to Molly Wesley the joy she so richly deserved. Hetty's poem in the *Gentleman's Magazine* for December, 1736, was a fitting expression of the family's grief in the passing of this lovely character.

Mehetabel, better known as Hetty, was next in the Wesley chronology. Her unique story deserves—and will be treated in—a separate chapter.

Anne, or Nancy, follows Hetty in the family line. The records furnish almost nothing about her except that she had the distinction of having made a happy marriage. Her husband, John Lambert, was a land surveyor in Epworth. He was apparently a well-educated man. It was he who carefully collected and preserved some of Samuel Wesley's early publications. He had a weakness for drink, a habit which was not helped by his association with Hetty's dissipated husband; but this was not serious enough to interfere with his and Nancy's happiness. After some years in Epworth, she and her husband moved to Hatfield, Hertfordshire. Their home was always open to Nancy's brothers John and Charles, and their visits proved a happy respite in their demanding schedule of itinerant preaching.

Martha, usually called Patty, was about four years younger than her brother John. She was strikingly like him in appearance. Their dispositions, too, were quite similar, and even their handwriting was almost identical. Martha was one of the most affectionate of all the Wesley children. She always moved

with the greatest deliberation and was possessed of a composure that nothing could disturb. Martha was lacking in the
ready wit of her brothers and sisters but was from childhood
serious and thoughtful. Susanna was well aware of her solemn
nature, as is illustrated by an incident related by Adam Clarke:

"One day, entering the nursery when all the children, Patty
excepted (who was ever sedate and reflecting), were in high
glee and frolic, the mother said, but not rebukingly, 'You will
all be more serious *one* day.' Martha . . . immediately said,
'Shall I be more serious, Mam?' 'NO,' replied the mother." [4]

There was a mutual attachment through their entire lives
between Martha and her brother John whom she so closely
resembled. He alone of all the children never joined in their
tricks to try to ruffle Patty.

Her mother was Martha's idol and constant companion
while the other children were at play. She sat at Susanna's
feet by the hour, eager to learn from her everything possible.
Martha was avid for knowledge and she was wise enough to
realize that Susanna's conversation could vastly enrich her
mind.

Martha was involved in various love affairs in her youth.
One of them was with John Romley, the schoolmaster who
also served for a time as curate to Samuel Wesley and as his
amanuensis for the book on *Job*. Romley had previously been
in love with Hetty, it should be added. It was lucky for
Martha that this romance did not ripen into marriage, for
Romley developed into a heavy drinker and came to a tragic
end.

Martha served for a time as a sort of companion in the
same family at Kelstein where Hetty was then employed.
Martha was not a success in this capacity, however, and soon
returned home. She made several visits to her uncle Matthew
Wesley in London, and at his invitation she went to live with
him and was a member of his household for a number of years.
Here she was given all the material comforts so sadly lacking

in the Epworth parsonage, but her uncle was by no means a religious man, and she missed the spiritual atmosphere of her own home. She sometimes visited her brother Samuel at Westminster, but her plain ways did not suit Samuel's wife, and so she made her visits less frequent.

There were several other young men, two of whom were friends of John Wesley, who paid court to Martha. While living in the home of her uncle Matthew, she met Westley Hall who had attended Oxford with her brothers John and Charles. He was a clergyman and supposedly of fine character and great promise. They became secretly engaged.

Meanwhile Mr. Hall was invited by John Wesley to accompany him to Epworth for a visit. While there Hall became enamored of Kezzy, the youngest of the Wesley daughters, the Epworth family all the while being entirely ignorant of his ties with Martha. Then he returned to London, and renewed his attentions to Martha. Early in 1735, they were married. Certainly they had Dr. Matthew Wesley's consent, for he gave Martha a handsome wedding present and made provision for her in his will. On the strength of Dr. Matthew Wesley's sanction, Susanna gave them her blessing also.

For several years all went well. Martha bore ten children to Mr. Hall, only one of whom survived infancy. Gradually her husband's true nature began to assert itself. He embraced first one faith and then another and was guilty of unfaithfulness to his wife. He had intimate relations with a seamstress who lived in the house as an employee of Martha's. The latter was entirely unsuspecting of the true state of affairs until the seamstress began to have labor pains and the servants apprised her of the true state of things. Mr. Hall immediately left home.

Martha made provision for the *accouchement,* then set out in search of her erring husband. She forgave him and persuaded him to return home.

Mr. Hall was so brutal to his only child that John and

Charles Wesley arranged to have the boy cared for away from home and assumed the expense of this care. The lad, who had great promise, died of smallpox at the age of fourteen.

Westley Hall not only spoke in favor of polygamy, he engaged in it himself and went off to the West Indies with a mistress, remaining there with her until her death.

After Martha's desertion by her husband she moved to London, and though she had a little property of her own, she was almost entirely dependent upon the kindness of her brothers. With all her trouble, she was never known to speak unkindly of her husband nor to bewail her fate. The wonder is that she could maintain her almost superhuman composure in the face of such dire tragedy. Perhaps her disposition was more phlegmatic than that of most people and her faith so firmly based that nothing could affect it. However that may be, she entered wholeheartedly into the work of the Methodist Societies in London and also took her place among the intellectuals of that city.

Because of her complete unselfishness and her amiable disposition she was much beloved by children. She had an enjoyable social life in London. After her brother Charles and his family moved to London she was often in their company, and their daughter Sarah was a great favorite with Martha. Dr. Samuel Johnson thought very highly of Martha and found her conversation informative and most stimulating. Indeed, he invited her to become a member of his household, along with several other friends. This she would not do but was often a guest at his table, discussing a wide variety of subjects, theology in particular.

Martha outlived all the rest of her large family, surviving her brother John by four months. When he died something went out of her, as if there were no longer anything to live for. Her niece, Sarah Wesley, who was with her when she died, had asked if she might be at her aunt's bedside in her last moments. Martha lived up to her true character in replying: "Yes, if you are able to bear it: but I charge you not to grieve more than half an hour."

In his will John Wesley left Mrs. Hall forty pounds to be paid out of the proceeds of the sale of his books after his death—the only property he had. She never lived to receive it. She bequeathed what little property she had to her beloved niece.

Quite fittingly, Martha Hall was interred in the same vault with her brother John in the burial ground behind John's City Road Chapel. Close they were in life, and in death they were not divided.

Kezziah Wesley, the only Wesley daughter who never married, was no less pathetic a figure than most of her sisters. From her birth soon after the fire until her death thirty-two years later she was never robust in health. Her great ambition always was to have a well cultivated mind, but repeated illness seems to have prevented the application to her studies that would have made this ambition possible. No historians mention her good looks, as they do with most of her sisters, and in a letter to her brother John, written in 1729, she shows her awareness of her lack in this regard.

Kezzey—the name by which she was affectionately called —at the age of eighteen, when Emilia was head teacher at a boarding school in Lincoln, secured a position there as part assistant and part pupil. She was given board and instruction as remuneration for her services, but she had no money for the clothes she needed to maintain her status and consequently went home. She was of a shy disposition and was frustrated by the hopeless poverty of her situation. Early she came to the belief that her life was to be a short one, and in her constant struggle to become resigned to her lot she often said that a life of celibacy was most fitting for her.

In the matter of Westley Hall's duplicity in his love affairs with Martha and Kezzy, neither of these sisters was at fault. It is difficult to understand how he could have proposed marriage to both without either sister having knowledge of his courtship of the other, but we must remember that communications in that day were very slow. The wonder is that Susanna should have been willing for either daughter to marry a man who was guilty of such a performance, and also that Martha should not have realized that happiness would be impossible with a man so fickle in his affections. Kezzy forgave him and the inference is that her love for him did not continue, since she lived with the Halls in their parsonage for several years.

When Samuel Wesley died and Epworth could no longer be the home of the family, Kezzy went to live with her brother Samuel. Later John Wesley made it possible for her to be a boarding guest in the home of Henry Piers, the Vicar of Bexley, and formerly a member of the Holy Club. She was happy there and John and Charles kept in as close touch with her as their arduous duties would permit. From historically accurate sources we learn that in her later years Kezzy was engaged to a gentleman with whom she was genuinely in love, but her death prevented their marriage. She died March 10, 1741, and her brother Charles was with her in her final hours.

There was always a particularly close bond between Kezzy and her brother Charles, similar to that between John and Patty. Charles was two years older than Kezzy, and he was especially protective of her in all her difficult experiences. In return, when Charles became dangerously ill in 1738, Kezzy left Bexley to nurse him. Her care of this beloved brother was evidently quite taxing for her frail constitution, for she herself fell ill immediately after his recovery.

The stories of most of the Wesley girls belong in the category of tragedy, some of it avoidable, some not. To attempt an analysis of the reasons behind the disasters of each would serve no purpose. Susanna suffered vicariously in the trials of them all; in some instances she was brought to her sickbed because of them.

The Wesley daughters never showed any jealousy of their brothers' superior advantages but took great pride in all their achievements. If at times the girls were more demanding of their brothers' time than they should have been, this must be attributed to the fact that their own lives were lived in an extremely narrow orbit.

It was strikingly evident in the later years of these children of Susanna that the love which characterized the family circle in the Epworth parsonage through all the vicissitudes of their sojourn there persisted long after Epworth ceased to be their home, indeed, as long as they all lived. No computer, however intricate, could figure out how the sons of that family were able to care for the varied needs of their sisters through the long years, but care for them they did, and for their children and their children's children when the need arose.

HETTY, WHO HAD SHOWN THE
GREATEST LITERARY PROMISE.

10
HETTY

Ordinarily, in a family of seven daughters conspicuous for
good looks, intelligence, and sprightliness, it would not be
possible to single out any one to take precedence over her
sisters. But in the case of the Wesley household even the most
reluctant historian would have to hand the palm to Mehetabel,
the fourth girl and first child to be born to Susanna after she
and Samuel arrived at Epworth.

Hetty, as she was familiarly called, was lavishly endowed
with gifts and graces. She was beautiful in face and form, her

117

mind was keen and facile. To add to these qualities, she was from childhood gay and good-humored, with a ready wit that made her attractive to young and old.

"Her fancy wit and genius often outran her judgment, and caused her parents both anxiety and trouble," [1] for her antics sometimes ran counter to the strict rules by which the Epworth parsonage operated. One might almost say it was a pity she was born to live in the eighteenth century when women were suppressed and supposed to be devoid of the individuality and means of self-expression which they now enjoy. Hetty Wesley did not easily fit into the mold proper for young ladies of her day.

The rector early recognized the unusual mental powers of his beautiful daughter and gave her the benefit of his best teaching. He was proud of her and her ability, at the tender age of eight, to read the Greek New Testament. She in turn delighted in serving as her father's amanuensis, and there was great intellectual congeniality between them.

As may well be imagined, Hetty's beauty and attractiveness won for her numerous beaus. Some of them were gay, frivolous young men who liked Hetty more for her good looks and her wit than for her more substantial qualities. Some of them she found unsuitable for life companionship; with others she was peremptorily forbidden to associate by parental edict. Hetty alluded to this frustrating state of affairs in some lines she sent to her mother:

> Pray speak a word in time of need,
> And with my sour-looked father plead
> For your distressèd daughter.

John Romley, former amanuensis and for a short time curate to the rector, in addition to his duties as a schoolmaster, was a suitor of Hetty's, but she was never deeply interested in him. However, her father took a hand in this affair also. He was convinced—and had reason to be—that Romley was not a suitable lover for Hetty. In his forthright fashion he broke up their correspondence and packed her off to Kelstein near Louth. There she served as governess to two small children in a home of wealth and comfort and was treated with the utmost kindness by her employers, Mr. and Mrs. Grantham.

It was at Kelstein that she met a young lawyer rated as "clever in his profession" and of "respectable family." [2] She fell madly in love with him. He dutifully asked the rector for Hetty's hand in marriage. But her father, after investigating into the young man's history, dubbed him an "unprincipled lawyer," refused his consent, and forbade Hetty to see him again. By this time Hetty had reached the age of twenty-seven and felt herself old enough to make her own decisions. Her father seemed to be always interfering in her love affairs, and this time she refused to give up her lover. After all she was now a mature woman earning her own living. And then since parental consent had been with finality withheld, her lover persuaded Hetty to elope with him, having given her every assurance that they were running away to be married. She spent one fateful night with him, but next morning, when the marriage was to take place, the bridegroom-to-be, living up to the reputation about which her father had warned, would not —certainly did not—go through with the ceremony. Hetty, a sadder and a wiser girl, had no alternative but to return home to Wroot to face the wrath of her scandalized parents. From then on until the last day of her life, dire and relentless tragedy was to be the fate of Hetty Wesley.

And who was the man with whom she ran away? Dr. V. H. Green in his *The Young Mr. Wesley* says his name was Will Attkins.[3] Though this name occurs several times in the annals of the Wesleys, there is not sufficient proof to establish the fact that Will Attkins was Hetty's lover. Some say that Hetty herself consistently refused to name the man who betrayed her.

One may picture the scene when Hetty reached home and

met her father. The strict code of an eighteenth-century divine, coupled with a Puritanical upbringing and his lack of understanding and sympathy where his girls were concerned, added up to an utter repudiation of Hetty and what she had done. Samuel would have ordered her from the house immediately but for Susanna's entreaties. There was also hurt pride with father Samuel. Such wantonness was a stain upon the spotless name of all the Annesleys and all the Wesleys, not to mention the reputation of Samuel himself as a highly respected clergyman of the Church of England. Besides, Hetty, who of all his daughters had shown the greatest literary promise, had defied his orders.

Any slightest regard for Hetty and the agony she was experiencing was completely lacking in Samuel. She had committed the unpardonable sin and had thereby placed herself beyond the bounds of parental love and solicitude.

It is no wonder then that Hetty, completely rejected and seeing no hope of even a tolerable existence at home, rashly vowed to marry the first man who asked her. Mary Wesley, her crippled sister, was the only member of the family who openly stood up to her father for Hetty's sake, and with sisterly concern she pleaded with Hetty not to go through with her awful vow. The rest of the family took no strong stand against Samuel in the matter. They felt, including Susanna, that Hetty was not truly repentant for what she had done, and by their lack of aggressiveness in her behalf acquiesced in Samuel's unforgiving attitude.

After all, he was an eighteenth-century *pater familias,* supreme in his command of his household. Susanna did remonstrate with him and wrote to her son John for advice on this problem.[4] John tried repeatedly to mollify his father, but it would have been earthshaking indeed to break into this uncompromising pattern of fatherly overlordship.

So Hetty kept her vow, in fact, she was forced to keep it by her father and mother acting together, and married William

Wright of Louth, an illiterate plumber who traveled through the country with his tools on his back, plying his trade.

There is a story to the effect that early in Hetty's acquaintance with Mr. Wright she realized that they were completely unsuited to each other and tried to back out of marrying him, but her father compelled her to go through with it.

Careful research reveals no record in this instance of Samuel's customary investigation into the credentials of his daughters' suitors. He was glad to get this sinful daughter off his hands and good riddance.

John Kirk says that Hetty left home after her father repudiated her, but no historians of the Wesley family give any account of where Hetty lived in the interval before she married Wright, whether perhaps she returned to her governess position with the Granthams, or whether she was allowed to remain at home. In the latter case it is reasonably certain that she did not come in contact with her father, for he never became truly reconciled to her. Her marriage to William Wright took place later in the year 1725.

Those who have followed closely the heartbreaking story of Hetty Wesley have always had good reason to suspect that she became pregnant as the result of the one unfortunate night with her lover, and that she gave birth to his baby. None of the historians of the Wesleys state this as a fact, even though they may have known it to be true—doubtless due to the prevalent reticence of that period regarding such delicate subjects, and also the desire to spare the famous Wesley family from any blot on its otherwise stainless scutcheon. However, they hint at it.

The Reverend John Kirk in *The Mother of the Wesleys,* referring to Hetty, observes cryptically: "It is in the power of our hand to lift the vail; but this allusion, which historic fidelity demanded, must suffice." [5] The "allusion" Kirk referred to is a quotation from a letter of Samuel Wesley to his brother Matthew Wesley, written in the third person shortly before Samuel's death: "If God has blessed him [meaning Samuel] with a numerous offspring, he has no reason to be ashamed of them, and if he had but that single one, it might have proved no support to his name or family."

Another reliable source, Eliza Clarke, writes in her book *Susanna Wesley:* "Hetty, who was a pretty, clever, sprightly girl, went wrong altogether, and was treated by both her parents with the harshness of rigid virtue that has never known temptation. They utterly refused to see or forgive her; and had not her brothers and uncle pitied and made allowances for her, her fate would have been even worse than it was." [6]

Furthermore, it may be asked, if pregnancy had not been involved in Hetty's tragic mistake, why would she have been so desperate as to make a marriage which, to a person of her keen intellect and fine sensibilities, could not be anything but utterly abhorrent? Even if her family had not been willing to welcome her back into the fold, certainly she knew that she could have maintained herself as a governess had there not been pregnancy as a complication. Surely, too, her uncle Matthew's home would have been open to her.

But if she were pregnant, her situation would, of course, be desperate indeed. In her day there were no havens for unwed mothers, nor adoption agencies where children born under such unhappy circumstances could be placed. The Wesley brothers, though they remonstrated with their father and sympathized with their "erring sister," as she was called, never dreamed of taking the decision regarding her out of their father's hands. Such defiance of a father's authority over his household would have been completely unthought of in the seventeen hundreds.

But in more recent days, Dr. Frank Baker, perhaps the greatest of the Wesleyan researchers, has established beyond question the truth about the paternity of Hetty's first child, that the "unprincipled lawyer" was indeed the father of this baby.

Dr. Baker has found a record in the manuscript Parish Register of the church at Haxey, a town not far from Epworth, of the marriage of Hetty Wesley to William Wright of Louth on October 13, 1725. Furthermore, the parish register at Louth records the baptism, on February 18, 1726, of "Mehetabell d. of William Wrightt." This same child was buried December 27, 1726, at Louth.

To complete this part of the story, it should be stated that everything points to the fact that Hetty's elopement took place early in May, 1725. George Stevenson says that she became acquainted with her lover early in 1725. John Kirk states that this young man asked Mr. Wesley for Hetty's hand in marriage in April, 1725.

When in May, 1725, Samuel Wesley, Jr. with his wife and child came to Wroot to see his parents, the visit was partly social, of course, but was partly for the purpose of straightening out with his father financial matters relating to the loans he had made to the rector for the education of John and Charles. Several authorities believe that another of his reasons for coming was to soften the rector's heart toward Hetty—a likely supposition since Samuel, Jr. involved himself in all the many crises of his family. That he was with his parents as early as May 10, 1725, is established by a letter written by Samuel, Sr. to his son John and dated May 10, 1725, which states: "Your brother Samuel, with his wife and child, are here".

Be that as it may, Dr. Baker's findings make all the facts regarding Hetty's indiscretion fall into place—her calamitous marriage in October to legitimize a baby she was expecting in less than four months, and the adamant attitude which her father maintained toward her to his dying day, adhering to a rigid code that had no place for the quality of mercy, even toward his favorite daughter.

For a time things went fairly well with Hetty and her husband. They lived at Louth where William Wright was connected with his father's plumbing business. It would be difficult to imagine a more pitiable adjustment than Hetty's to life with a man like William Wright. But from the very beginning of her marriage she determined to make him happy at whatever cost to herself. She had made a tragic mistake which nothing could undo. She would atone for it the rest of her life by being a dutiful and affectionate wife, in spite of the disparity of their tastes and background. This she did. She could have no romantic love for her husband, but she liked him and meticulously looked after his interests.

There were times when Hetty's desire to see her family was overwhelming. After all, she had never before been separated from them, except for her short period of employment with the Granthams, and her stay with her uncle Matthew Wesley following the fire. A few days with her mother and Mary she felt she must have, and she desperately longed for her father's forgiveness that she might be back on the old familiar footing with him. Accordingly, she made the short journey to Wroot but returned to her own home more brokenhearted than before. Her sister Mary reports on her visit in a letter to Charles Wesley at Oxford:

"My unhappy sister was at Wroot the week after you left us, where she stayed two or three days, and returned to Louth without seeing my father. I must stop for when I think of her misfortunes, I may say with Edgar, 'O fortune . . .' "

Not long after her visit Hetty gave birth to her second child, a son, but it lived only a few days.

During the summer of 1726, John was at home assisting his father. Repeatedly he argued with Samuel about his treatment of Hetty but to no avail. On August 28 of that summer, after due consideration, he preached a sermon at Wroot on the topic: "Universal Charity," or "Charity Due to Wicked Persons." The sermon was aimed directly at his father who with Susanna quickly recognized the fact. Samuel was greatly hurt and discussed the matter with Charles.

"Every day," said Samuel, "you hear how he [John] contradicts me and takes your sister's part before my face, nay he disputes with me. . . ."

Charles retailed this conversation to John, and the latter and his father became reconciled with tears and with the promise on John's part that he would help his father with the ever-present *Dissertations on the Book of Job*.

Samuel's attitude toward poor Hetty was little changed as a result of the sermon. In a letter to Samuel, Jr., written August 29, 1726, John says:

"My sister Hetty's behaviour has, for aught I have heard, been innocent enough since her marriage; most of my disputes on charity with my father were on her account, he being inconceivably exasperated against her. 'Tis likely enough he would not see her (Hetty) when at Wroot; he has disowned her long ago. He never spoke of her in my hearing but with the utmost detestation; both he and my mother and several of my sisters were persuaded her penitence was all feigned. One great reason for my writing the above-mentioned sermon was to endeavour as far as in me lay, to convince them that even on the supposition that she was impenitent, some tenderness was due to her still which my mother, when I read it to her, was so well aware of that she told me as soon as I had read it, 'You writ this sermon for Hetty. . . .' "

An unpublished letter from Martha Wesley to her brother John, dated February 7, 1727, reports that her father had been to see Hetty "who by good providence was brought to bed two days before he got thither, which perhaps might prevent his saying what he otherwise might have said to her; for none that deserves the name of a man would say anything to grieve a woman in a condition where grief is often present death to them. . . . Sister Hetty's child is dead."

By this time things were not going well with Hetty's marriage in spite of her desperate efforts to please her husband. Uncle Matthew Wesley gave her five hundred pounds as a sort of wedding gift, and with this sum William Wright was able to set up his own business as plumber and glazier in London. There Hetty and William established themselves at Mr. Wakenden's in Crown Court, Dean's Street, near Soho, William's shop being on the same premises. Charles Wesley in a letter to John, dated January 1, 1728, reports having visited them there recently for the first time.

Hetty entertained a forlorn hope that this improvement in her husband's business would make for their greater happiness, but such was not to be. William Wright loved Hetty after his fashion, but he was a weak character and what started out to be moderate tippling became a confirmed habit. Perhaps a contributing factor to his drinking lay in a realization of the irremediable difference between Hetty's station in life and his own, despite her efforts to please him. At any rate, he spent more and more evenings in taverns with unsavory companions. Her days were filled with worry over her husband's debts and the loss of business which his increased drinking had brought about, and night after night she lay awake, wondering in what condition he would return to her. There were times in his drunken state that he was a veritable beast, even to the point of striking her.

Hetty expressed herself in some tragic lines which, though not outstanding as poetry, reveal dramatically the agony through which she was passing:

> The ardent lover cannot find
> A coldness in his fair unkind,
> But blaming what he cannot hate,
> He mildly chides the dear ingrate,
> And though despairing of relief,
> In soft complaining vents his grief.
> Then what should hinder but that I,

Impatient of my wrongs, may try,
By saddest softest strains, to move
My wedded, latest, dearest love,
To throw his cold neglect aside,
And cheer once more his injured bride?

O thou, whom sacred rites designed
My guide, and husband ever kind,
My sovereign master, best of friends,
On whom my earthly bliss depends;
If e'er thou didst in Hetty see
Aught fair, or good, or dear to thee,
If gentle speech can ever move
The cold remains of former love,
Turn thee at last—my bosom ease,
Or tell me why I cease to please.

Is it because revolving years,
Heart-breaking sighs, and fruitless tears,
Have quite deprived this form of mine
Of all that once thou fanciedst fine?
Ah no! what once allured thy sight
Is still in its meridian height.
These eyes their usual lustre show
When uneclipsed by flowing woe.
Old age and wrinkles in this face
As yet could never find a place:
A youthful grace informs these lines,
Where still the purple current shines,
Unless, by thy ungentle art,
It flies to aid my wretched heart:
Nor does this slighted bosom show
The thousand hours it spends in woe.

Or is it that, oppressed with care,
I stun with loud complaints thine ear;
And make thy home, for quiet meant
The seat of noise and discontent?
Ah no! those ears were ever free
From matrimonial melody:

For though thine absence I lament
When half the lonely night is spent,
Yet when the watch or early morn
Has brought me hopes of thy return,
I oft have wiped these watchful eyes,
Concealed my cares, and curbed my sighs,
In spite of grief, to let thee see
I wore an endless smile for thee.

Had I not practised every art
T'oblige, divert, and cheer thy heart,
To make me pleasing in thine eyes,
And turn thy house to paradise;
I had not asked, "Why dost thou shun
These faithful arms, and eager run
To some obscure, unclean retreat,
With fiends incarnate glad to meet,
The vile companions of thy mirth,
The scum and refuse of the earth;
Who, when inspired by beer, can grin
At witless oaths and jests obscene,
Till the most learned of the throng
Begins a tale of ten hours long;
While thou, in raptures, with stretched jaws
Crownest each joke with loud applause?"

Deprived of freedom, health, and ease,
And rivalled by such things as these;
This latest effort will I try,
Or to regain thy heart, or die.
Soft as I am, I'll make thee see
I will not brook contempt from thee!

Then quit the shuffling doubtful sense,
Nor hold me longer in suspense;
Unkind, ungrateful, as thou art,
Say, must I ne'er regain thy heart?
Must all attempts to please thee prove
Unable to regain thy love?

If so, by truth itself I swear,

The sad reverse I cannot bear:
No rest, no pleasure, will I see;
My whole of bliss is lost with thee!
I'll give all thoughts of patience o'er;
(A gift I never lost before);
Indulge at once my rage and grief,
Mourn obstinate, disdain relief,
And call that wretch my mortal foe,
Who tries to mitigate my woe;
Till life, on terms severe as these,
Shall, ebbing, leave my heart at ease;
To thee thy liberty restore
To laugh when Hetty is no more.[7]

The last lingering hope Hetty had for binding her husband
to her was through their children, but one after another of her
babies died before they could even register their personality.
She was of the firm opinion that the loss of her babies was
caused by the lead fumes issuing from her husband's shop. Her
third child was born September 25, 1728, and died three days
afterward. William Wright reports the sad news to John
Wesley at Oxford where the latter was then a Fellow:

"This comes to Let you know that my wife is brought to bed
and is in a hopeful way of Doing well but the Dear child died—the
Third day after it was born—which has been of great concerne to
me and my wife She joyns With me In Love to your Selfe and
Bro: Charles

From Your Loveing Bro:
to Comnd—Wm Wright.

P.S. Ive sen you Sum Verses that my wife maid of Dear Lamb
Let me hear from one or both of you as Soon as you think
Conveniant."

The verses which were dictated to her husband were composed during Hetty's confinement. The orthography has been
corrected.

A Mother's Address to Her Dying Infant
(by Mrs. Wright)

Tender softness! infant mild!
Perfect, sweetest, loveliest child!
Transient lustre! beauteous clay!
Smiling wonder of a day!
Ere the last convulsive start
Rends thy unresisting heart;
Ere the long-enduring swoon
Weigh thy precious eyelids down;
Ah, regard a mother's moan,
Anguish deeper than thy own.

Fairest eyes, whose dawning light
Late with rapture blest my sight,
Ere your orbs extinguished be,
Bend their trembling beams on me!
Drooping sweetness! verdant flower!
Blooming, withering in an hour!
Ere thy gentle breast sustains
Latest, fiercest, mortal pains,
Hear a suppliant! let me be
Partner in thy destiny!

This poem was printed long afterward by John in the *Arminian Magazine*.[8]

By the time Hetty had lost her fourth child in infancy she had reached a point of utter despair. She had tried by every means in her power to make herself attractive to her husband and win him from his evil ways. Now it appeared that there would never be any children to make their appeal to his fatherly instincts. Increasingly she felt that she must be under God's curse and that nothing she might do to redeem the past would avail with Him. There was always with her the old regard for her father's opinion and a longing for his forgiveness which had never yet been granted her. In this spirit she wrote to

Samuel Wesley, and the following letters set forth the shocking interchange between them:

From Hetty to Her Father (undated)

Honoured Sir, although you have cast me off, and I know that a determination once taken by you is not easily moved, I must tell you that some word of your forgiving is not only necessary to me, but would make happier the marriage in which, as you compelled it, you must still (I think) feel no small concern. My child, on whose frail help I had counted to make our life more supportable to my husband and myself, is dead. Should God give and take away another, I can never escape the thought that my father's intercession might have prevailed against His wrath, which I shall then, alas! take to be manifest.

Forgive me, sir, that I make you a party in such happiness (or unhappiness) as the world generally allows to be, under God, a portion for two. But as you planted my matrimonial bliss, so you cannot run away from my prayer when I beseech you to water it with a little kindness. My brothers will report to you what they have seen of my way of life and my daily struggle to redeem the past. But I have come to a point where I feel your forgiveness to be necessary to me. I beseech you, then, not to withhold it.

Mehet. Wright [9]

The Answer (undated)

Daughter—If you would persuade me that your penitence is more than feigned, you are going the wrong way to work. I decline to be made a party to your matrimonial fortunes, as you claim in what appears to be intended for the flower of your letter; and in your next, if you would please me, I advise you to display less wit and more evidence of honest self-examination. To that—which is the beginning of repentance—you do not appear to have attained. Yet it would teach you that your troubles, if you have any, flow from your own sin, and that for any inconveniences you may find in marriage you are probably as much to blame (at the very least) as your honest husband. Your brothers speak well of him, and I shall always think myself obliged to him for his civilities to you.

But what are your troubles? You do not name them. What hurt has matrimony done you? *I know only that it has given you a good name* [italics mine]. I do not remember that you were used to have so frightful an idea of it as you have now. Pray be more explicit. Restrain your wit if you wish to write again, and I will answer your next if I like it.

Your father,
S. Wesley[10]

And this was the man who wrote a *Life of Our Lord Jesus Christ*—wrote it in verse and with scholarly precision too! But how he missed the tender spirit of forgiveness that shone through every facet of the Master's life! For Samuel Wesley reflected not one iota of such compassion in his treatment of his own daughter in her hour of greatest need.

Hetty's reply to her father, dated London, July 3, 1729:

Honoured Sir—Though I was glad, on any terms, of the favour of a line from you, yet I was concerned at your displeasure on account of the unfortunate paragraph which you are pleased to say was meant for the flower of my letter. . . . I wish it had not gone, since I perceive it gave you some uneasiness.

But since what I said occasioned some queries, which I should be glad to speak freely about, . . . I earnestly beg that the little I shall say may not be offensive to you, since I promise to be as little witty as possible, though I can't help saying you only accuse me of being too much so; especially these late years past I have been pretty free from that scandal.

You ask me what hurt matrimony has done me, and whether I had always so frightful an idea of it as I have now. Home questions indeed! and I once more beg of you not to be offended at the least I can say to them, if I say nothing.

I had not always such notions of wedlock as now, but thought that where there was a mutual affection and desire of pleasing, something near an equality of mind and person, either earthly or heavenly wisdom, and anything to keep love warm between a young couple, there was a possibility of happiness in a married state; but when all, or most of these, were wanting, I ever thought people could not marry without sinning against God and themselves. . . .

You are so good to my spouse and me as to say you shall always think yourself obliged to him for his civilities to me. I hope he will always continue to use me better than I merit from him in one respect.

I think exactly the same of my marriage as I did before it happened [italics mine]; but though I would have given at least one of my eyes for the liberty of throwing myself at your feet before I was married at all, yet since it is past, and matrimonial grievances are usually irreparable, I hope you will condescend to be so far of my opinion as to own that, since upon some accounts I am happier than I deserve, it is best to say little of things quite past remedy, and endeavour, as I really do, to make myself more and more contented, though things may not be to my wish. . . .

Though I cannot justify my late indiscreet letter, . . . yet I need not remind you that I am not more than human, and if the calamities of life . . . sometimes wring a complaint from me, I need tell no one that though I bear I must feel them. And if you cannot forgive what I have said, I sincerely promise never more to offend you by saying too much; which (with begging your blessing) is all from your most obedient daughter,

Mehetabel Wright [11]

Samuel Wesley's answer to Hetty's second letter, if there was one, has been lost. It was quite clear, however, that there was little hope that father Samuel would ever change his rigid attitude toward her. Cut off then irrevocably from her childhood home and the loved ones there, she would have been entirely alone in her grief had it not been for other members of the family who tried in every way they knew to soften her tragic lot. Her brother Samuel helped her as far as his meager means would allow, and she visited in his home at Westminster, being careful always not to antagonize Mrs. Samuel Wesley, Jr., whose tart tongue had upon several occasions lashed out against some member of her husband's family. Charles went to see Hetty often at her lodgings in Soho, and also John whenever he had opportunity.

It is good to know that her uncle Matthew Wesley took her with him to Bath and Tunbridge, and she spent much time at his house where she associated with people of note in the literary world of London. In these circles she was held in high esteem. Hetty would never collect her writings in a single volume, but some of them may be found in various publications: *The Gentleman's Magazine, The Poetical Register, The Christian Magazine,* and *The Arminian Magazine.* Many of her writings which she sent to members of the family were lost.

A number of authorities believe that Hetty was the author of all, or part of, *The Hymn of Eupolis to the Creator.* This has been ascribed to Samuel Wesley and is considered one of his finest writings. However, a large part of the original of this poem was in Hetty's handwriting, with the editing in Samuel's.

Hetty kept in close contact with her uncle Matthew as long as he lived. She faithfully nursed him through long periods of illness, and finally, in 1737, he died in her arms. His will, dated February 8, 1735, bequeathed to Hetty two hundred pounds and to his great-niece, Amelia Wright, a hundred pounds. This last bequest shows that one of Hetty's children survived early infancy at least, but how long the child lived is not known.

Dr. Matthew Wesley's only son was a great disappointment to his father. He was educated at Oxford but lived a profligate life. He finally went to India and never returned to his father's house. Most of Dr. Matthew Wesley's estate was left to his sister, Mrs. Dyer, and after her lifetime to his son, but historians of the Wesley family fail to record whether the son ever returned to claim this money.

The name of Susanna is conspicuously absent from any

record of members of the family who visited Hetty after her marriage. Why did Susanna, the devoted mother, never once go to Hetty in her times of distress? The only plausible explanation for her failure here is that Susanna was torn between love for her daughter and what has been called her "conscientious refusal to countenance her." More important than that, Susanna was bound by Samuel's stern command which would forbid any contact with this rejected daughter. It is believed that Susanna's inner conflict over Hetty had much to do with her near fatal illness during the period which she called her "sad defection when I was almost without hope."

Mary's death in 1734 was a great sorrow to Hetty, doubly so because she had been cut off from all communication with this beloved sister.

Historians of Samuel Wesley make no mention of Hetty's presence at Epworth when her father died. He would not have wanted her there. But when Susanna took up residence with John in 1739 for the last years of her life, Hetty had once more the joy of companionship with her mother and the comfort that Susanna more than anyone else could give her. By this time the five remaining Wesley daughters were all living in or near London, so that the family group must often have gathered in Susanna's quarters.

For a long time William Wright placed severe limitations upon his wife's religious activities, and like a dutiful wife of her day she obeyed his commands. Later he softened his attitude in this regard, and she became a Methodist. John speaks of receiving help in the work of God for a short time from Hetty, "of whom I should least have expected it."

After Susanna's death there began a noticeable decline in Hetty's health. The trials and sufferings of her unhappy life were taking their toll. Those who were dearest to her, her mother, Mary, and uncle Matthew, had gone, and she must continue alone her struggle for the inner peace and assurance she had for some time so fervently desired. Hetty was too honest a person to claim something she had not really received, and her spiritual trek was a long and difficult one. Her letter to John, dated Stanmore, 1743, is most revealing:

Dear Brother, . . . After I was convinced of sin and of your opinions, as far as I had examined your principles, I still forebore declaring my sentiments as openly as I had an inclination to do, fearing I should relapse into my former state. When I was delivered from this fear, and had a blessed hope that He who had begun would finish His work, I never confessed so powerfully as I ought how entirely I was of your mind, because I was taxed with insincerity and hypocrisy whenever I opened my mouth in favour of religion, or owned how great things God had done for me.

This discouraged me utterly, and prevented me from making my change so public as my folly and vanity had formerly been. But now my health is gone I cannot be easy without declaring that I have long desired to know one thing, Jesus Christ and Him crucified, and this desire prevails above all others.

And though I am cut off from all human help or ministry, I am not without assistance; though I have no spiritual friend, nor ever had one yet, except perhaps once in a year or two, when I have seen one of my brothers or some other religious person by stealth, yet (no thanks to me) I am enabled to seek Him still, and to be satisfied with nothing else than God, in whose presence I affirm this truth. I dare not desire health, only patience, resignation, and the spirit of an healthful mind. I have been so long weak that I know not how long my trial may last, but I have a firm persuasion and blessed hope (though no full assurance) that in the country I am going to I shall not sing "Hallelujah!" and "Holy, holy, holy!" without company, as I have done in this.[12]

By this time her husband seems to have permitted Hetty to travel from home more than formerly. So by arrangement of her brothers she went to the famous Spa at Bristol in search of health. While there she was nursed by a Mrs. Vigor, and the other Methodists of that quite Methodist city poured out upon her the warm friendship she had lacked for so many years. She returned home somewhat better but was still unable to attend to her household duties and was confined to bed most of the time.

For the last years of her life Hetty was an invalid. Charles Wesley was often with her and at the same time tried to strengthen William Wright's efforts to reform.

As the end was approaching, Hetty remarked to a friend: "I have long ardently wished for death, because, you know, we Methodists always die in a transport of joy." Her extreme suffering at the end denied her this experience—there was to be no ecstasy for Hetty even in death. By strange coincidence it was while London was in a state of great alarm over a series of earthquakes that the turbulent life of Hetty Wesley came to an end. The date was March 21, 1750, and she was but fifty-three years of age. Charles alone, of her brothers and sisters, followed her to her grave.

After Hetty's death, Charles Wesley was often with William Wright trying to help him find a faith he had not yet known. In his queer way, William Wright had loved Hetty, but he was of too coarse a fiber to understand the refinement of her nature. He married again, but Hetty was the love of his life. Faithful Charles Wesley was with him in his final hours and firmly believed that at the last William Wright was penitent.

Where Hetty Wesley is buried is not known. She wrote her own pathetic epitaph, but it was never graven on her headstone.

Hers was the tragedy of a blithe spirit broken by her own impetuous nature and the strictures of the time in which she lived. But there is more than that to Hetty's story. It is the triumph also of that spirit. By the time she reached middle life, her wilfulness had long given place to the enduring fortitude that adversity not infrequently brings about in a man or woman. Hetty Wesley's life was a tragedy, yes, but it was also a triumph—the triumph of a human spirit refined in the crucible of unremitting sorrow and rejection.

JOHN, CHARLES, AND SAMUEL—
FRANK DISAGREEMENT BUT NEVER
ANY DIMINUTION OF LOVE.

11
THE
SONS

When we review the lives of the three Wesley boys, it would seem highly inappropriate here to write at length about John and Charles, the more famous of Susanna's sons. Public libraries and those in the homes of Methodists the world over proudly display on their shelves biographies of these noted founders of Methodism which analyze the sons of Susanna from many points of view. Indeed, historians are still busily searching for any chance letter or record that will throw more light upon their lives. Treatment of them in these pages, therefore, will be confined chiefly to their relationships with their parents, with each other, and with the rest of the family.

The ties between John Wesley and his mother were very close. The greatest influence in his life was, without question, Susanna. From his father he inherited a certain sturdiness of fiber, both physical and spiritual, that stood him in good stead during the strenuous program of his later life. To his father, too, he owed his early training in the classics and in other branches of learning in which his Oxonian parent was so proficient. John remembered through the years many words of profound wisdom he got from Samuel Wesley, an example of which he quoted thirty-five years after it was given:

"Child, you think to carry everything by dint of argument. But you will find by and by, how little is ever done in the world by clear wisdom."

But when all is said and done, John was his mother's own child, so like her in temperament, so unruffled and deliberate in judgment. His incisive, logical mind he owed to her, with a certain practicality thrown in. One of the outstanding traits of his genius was his ability to systematize both his personal life and that of the followers he drew after him. This methodical trait was a direct outgrowth of his mother's training, and even the name Methodist, given to the movement, is a reminder of this fact.

Wesley's *Journal,* the master text for all students of Methodism, is a product of Susanna's insistence upon rigid self-examination. In this *Journal* he set down each night what he had done that day, not simply for record, but with an eye to examining what had been accomplished and bettering that day's performance at a future time.

It is an amazing trait of John Wesley's that he eagerly sought his parents' advice, even after he had reached maturity. When he was already a member of the Holy Club at Oxford he would not enter into a visitation ministry to the Oxford prisoners until he had gained his father's sanction. Since Samuel and Samuel's father before him had preached to the prisoners during Oxford days, approval was not long in coming: "Go on, then, in God's name, in the path to which your Saviour has directed you, and that track wherein your father has gone before you."

It is no wonder that when to such a background there was added to John Wesley the compelling power of his cataclysmic Aldersgate experience, he could awaken all England from its religious apathy and influence the course of history as few men of his generation.

Even after his life was entirely given over to the movement that he started, the ties of John Wesley's family circle were as strong as ever, and the personal needs of its various members were his constant concern. It was he who provided a home for his mother in her last years, and also for several of his sisters. It was he who directed and largely paid for the education of his unfortunate sisters' children, not to mention the support of young Westley Hall until his untimely death, a responsibility he shared with his brother Charles.

In the providence of God, John Wesley was the last survivor of the Wesley household except for Martha whose death occurred about four months after his. He passed away at the age of eighty-seven, having preached his last sermon just one week before.

A marble medallion of John Wesley with his brother Charles is ensconced in Westminster Abbey with the rest of England's great. Books upon books have been written on every facet of John Wesley's genius. "But in the case of a man like Wesley, panegyric is out of place," writes Luke Tyerman. "He is one of the very few, whose memory can afford to do without it. His well-won and world-wide fame requires no inscription on his monumental marble . . . more elaborate than this:

John Wesley
Born, A.D. 1703
Died A.D. 1791"

Charles Wesley, "of the merry eye and the warm heart," was like John short in stature but heavier than his wiry brother. The two men were completely different in temperament, but their unfailing love and respect for each other made of them a splendid team in the building of Methodism.

Charles was quick-tempered and abrupt in manner like his father, contrasted with the quiet forcefulness of his brother John. There was no dearth of courage in either of them.

John was the dominant leader and organizer, and Charles preferred it so; but Charles with his wit and vivacity instinctively drew people to him, for he was made for friendship. He understood men and their motives much better than did John Wesley and thereby saved his brother many a pitfall.

In Charles Wesley's early life, particularly during his first year at Oxford, his brother John thought that he did not take his religion seriously enough and told him so. "What!" was the jocular reply, "Would you have me be a saint all at once?" Later Charles wrote to John: "It is owing, in a great measure, to somebody's prayers—my mother's most likely—that I am come to think as I do; for I can not tell myself how or when I woke out of my lethargy."

It was really Charles Wesley who started the Holy Club; but when John returned to Oxford from his curacy at Epworth and Wroot and joined this group, it was he who at once became its unquestioned leader.

These two brothers were more than ordinarily close, at Oxford, on the expedition to Georgia, and, after their conversion, in the spread of the Methodist movement. Through the long strenuous years together as itinerant preachers they were amazingly at one. Though they differed at times, their devotion was such that each yielded to the other on occasion, making an unusual equanimity of effort in the work which was then the ruling passion of both their lives. It is not by accident that the Wesley memorial in the Abbey portrays the profiles of the two brothers side by side, for they were truly a team.

The preaching of the two men was quite different. John Wesley was no orator like George Whitefield, but he preached with almost a prophetic voice and with the authority of one who knew himself to be the spokesman of Almighty God. His words seared into the very depths of the uncouth folk, who chiefly made up his audiences, with a convicting power that was almost miraculous. The logical reasoning behind this preaching was John Wesley's, and the dynamic personality was his, but the power was of the Holy Spirit, and unprecedented things happened as a result.

Charles Wesley's preaching was of a different sort. "In the prime of life," observes William Fitchett, "he was a preacher of almost unsurpassed power, talking in sentences that had the rush and impact of bullets, but which vibrated with electric thrills of emotion. . . . He felt truth rather than reasoned about it, and his feelings were wiser than his reasoned beliefs."

In 1749, Charles Wesley married Miss Sarah Gwynne of Garth, Wales, the daughter of Marmaduke Gwynne, a well-to-do magistrate. It proved to be a happy marriage, and of this union two sons and a daughter survived their parents. The sons, Charles and Samuel, were talented musicians, and both developed into organists of note. However, neither of them had any sympathy for Methodism, and Samuel even became a Roman Catholic. Charles Wesley's daughter Sally was a great favorite with her aunt Martha. It was Sally Wesley who gave to Adam Clarke many facts about the Wesleys which he used in his book *Memoirs of the Wesley Family.*

Charles Wesley's wife suffered an attack of smallpox which permanently marred her beauty, but in the eyes of her adoring husband she was always beautiful. Mrs. Charles Wesley was with John Wesley when he died.

In 1756, Charles practically retired from his itinerant activity. His health had been bad for years—the chief reason he did not return to Georgia. Besides, there were disagreements with John over policy, and, lastly, the demanding schedule of an itinerant preacher was not conducive to a happy married life. So he settled down with his family in Bristol. However, he continued to make preaching missions to various parts of England, particularly in the West, and preached regularly in Bristol. But from 1756 on, John bore the lonely load of leadership without his beloved brother beside him. During this period in his life, however, Charles was still making a significant contribution to the cause of Methodism through his leadership in the work at Bristol, then one of the three major centers of the Methodist movement.

Charles Wesley was always greatly influenced by his older brother Samuel who had been almost like a second father to his youngest brother. Sammy had supported him while at Westminster and had guided his studies there. It was largely through his efforts that Charles was able to enter Oxford. But Samuel Wesley II was strictly a High Churchman to the end of his life and thoroughly disapproved of the Methodists. Partly because of this, Charles Wesley as he grew older developed a strange inconsistency. He had preached in the fields with all the fervor of a Methodist evangelist; but as the Methodist movement progressed, the emotional manifestations that followed some of the preaching revolted his sensibilities and filled him with fear for the future of the cause.

In later years, partly in the interest of securing better musical opportunities for his sons, he moved from Bristol to London, to John's delight. He preached chiefly in Methodism's City Road Chapel but took John's place during his absences from London in overseeing the ever growing work of the London area. But Charles made it crystal clear that he was not to be buried in the Chapel churchyard at City Road, since it was to him unconsecrated ground. He died March 29, 1788, after ten years of infirmity and was laid to rest in the Parish Burying Ground in Marylebone, London. It is interesting to note that only Church of England clergymen were asked to serve as pallbearers!

Charles Wesley's real contribution—and it was to the whole Christian world—was as a hymn writer, perhaps the greatest of all time. His was the blending of deep religious insight with a poetic genius infused by classical learning and wide reading. Anywhere and everywhere he was forever composing hymns —in a room with people talking all around him; on horseback as he rode from one preaching engagement to another, the very rhythm of the horse's hoofbeats finding their way into the cadences of his lines.

It was John Wesley who largely fashioned the theology of the Methodists, but Charles wove it into their very being with his hymns. "He set the masses singing," as Bishop Charles Wesley Flint expressed it, along the highways, in lowly homes, and in the kirk. Nor were these hymns limited to Methodism. In hymn books of every Christian denomination Charles Wesley's hymns have found a place—"Jesus, Lover of My Soul," "Christ the Lord Is Risen Today," "Hark! the Herald Angels Sing," "O for a Thousand Tongues to Sing," and scores of others. His songs belong to the ages.

After Charles Wesley's death, John Wesley on one occasion was lining out to a congregation his brother's famous hymn: "Come, O Thou Traveler Unknown," called "Wrestling Jacob." When he came to the couplet

> My company before is gone,
> And I am left alone with thee,

the old man could go on no further but stopped, covered his face, and wept.

The poetic genius of Charles Wesley did not end with him. His sons have been mentioned. His grandson Samuel Sebastian Wesley, son of Samuel, became one of the greatest organists of the Church of England and a composer as well. The tune "Aurelia" to which we sing "The Church's One Foundation" was his composition.

Samuel Wesley, Jr., classicist, poet, teacher, clergyman, humanitarian, might have occupied a more important spot in English history had he not been eclipsed by the eminence of his younger brothers. After he left home at fourteen for Westminster school in London, young Samuel was never again a member of the Epworth parsonage. But his parents kept in close touch with him through frequent letters, advising him, as they did his brothers at a later date, on many matters regarding his religious as well as his physical well-being. He was receptive to their words of wisdom, and there is no record of any conflicts on the part of Sammy with either his father or his mother.

There was always a substantial quality about this oldest son of Susanna and Samuel. Through the years he stood solidly behind them in whatever calamity befell them—and there were many.

He early showed a special interest in the classics. His father laid the groundwork for these studies before he sent him off to Westminster School. The school had a reputation for excellent teaching in this field, and young Samuel from the first showed great proficiency in classical learning. In his third year he had the honor of becoming a King's Scholar, which carried with it welcome financial advantages. While still a pupil at Westminster, Sammy was chosen, of all the scholars, to read to Bishop Sprat in the evenings. Most young men would have considered this a signal honor; but young Samuel was full of resentment because this chore took him away from his own studies which he considered more important. "He chose me from all the scholars," wrote Sammy to his father; "me who am both hoarse and short-sighted." The letter, incidentally, was written in Latin.

From Westminster he went on to Christ Church, Oxford, and received a Master's degree in a short time. From Oxford he returned to Westminster as usher (teacher) and remained in that capacity for twenty years. Shortly after his return to Westminster he took Holy Orders. He was ordained by Bishop Atterbury, then Dean of Westminster and Bishop of Rochester, but Samuel, though ordained, continued in the role of educator until his untimely death at the age of forty-nine.

Out of the first salary he received as an usher he sent home a portion to help with the family finances, and as long as he lived he continued to share his income with his father and mother, an income that was never large. As soon as Charles Wesley was ready for Westminster School, Samuel, Jr. assumed the expenses of his schooling and directed his courses until he, too, was made a King's Scholar. Samuel also helped John financially with his education. He permitted no mention to be made of any help he gave to his family, therefore much of it passed unnoticed.

In 1715, Mr. Samuel Wesley, Jr. married Ursula, the daughter of the Reverend John Berry, then his near neighbor at Westminster. It was a happy marriage, though his sisters and brothers found their sister-in-law a bit waspish. It must be said to her credit, however, that she went along with her husband in the contributions to the Epworth exchequer that had become by now a regular part of his life.

As a man of letters, the younger Samuel moved in the circle of Pope, Swift, Addison, and Prior, and enjoyed a fine reputation as a wit, a poet, and a thorough scholar. He was the author of many beautiful hymns which were formerly sung in English congregations of various denominations, but it is Charles's matchless hymn writing, not Samuel's, that has survived the test of two centuries. As a satirist Samuel was preeminent, and his facile pen, when turned against those political figures of the day of whom he disapproved, could cut with the sharpness of a razor. An oft-quoted example of Samuel's devastating wit are the lines on the erection of a monument to the poet Samuel Butler, author of *Hudibras:*

> While Butler, needy wretch! was yet alive,
> No purse-proud printer would a dinner give:
> See him, when starved to death, and turned to dust,
> Presented with a monumental bust!
> The Poet's fate is here in emblem shown:
> He asked for *bread,* and he received a *stone.*[1]

His interests extended far beyond the classroom and study, however. It was largely through his long and patient efforts that the hospital at Hyde Park Corner, now known as St. George's Hospital, was erected.

He had his own way of taking care of situations he thought needed remedying. In London he was a frequent guest in the home of Lord Oxford, a patron of letters. Upon each departure from Lord Oxford's home the liveried servants lined up at the door expecting a gratuity. Mr. Wesley grew weary of this custom which he considered presumptuous, and on one occasion he paused at the head of the line and announced in positive tones that he would tip them once a month but no more. His action helped to break up this obnoxious procedure.

It is amazing how closely allied Sammy remained with the daily life of the Epworth parsonage after his separation from it. The following lines from one of his poems illustrate this:

> Methinks I see you striving all
> Who first shall answer to his call,
> Or lusty Anne, or feeble Moll,
> Sage Pat, or sober Hetty;
> To rub his cassock's draggled tail,
> Or reach his hat from off the nail,
> Or seek the key to draw his ale

When damsel haps to steal it.
To burn his pipe, or mend his clothes,
Or nicely darn his russet hose—
For comfort of his aged toes—
So fine they cannot feel it.[2]

Though Sammy was, in his father's words, "a father to your brothers and sisters," and loved them all devotedly, he was very positive in his opinions regarding what they did. He never wanted either of his brothers to go to Georgia and believed Charles completely unsuited to the position of secretary to General Oglethorpe on that American expedition. Later events proved he was right. His estimate of Westley Hall was unfavorable from the start, and again his judgment was correct. In a letter to his brother Charles, dated September 21, 1726, he writes: "There was no great likelihood of his being a favorite with me: his tongue is too smooth for my roughness and rather inclines me to suspect than believe."

The younger Samuel Wesley was a Tory, a High Churchman and an intense Jacobite, and he never modified by a hair his adherence to any of these persuasions. In 1722, his patron Bishop Atterbury was accused of trying to bring back the Pretender to the English throne. The bishop was sent to the Tower and afterward banished forever from his native land. Samuel Wesley, Jr. never believed Bishop Atterbury guilty of this charge though facts uncovered after the bishop's death proved Samuel's opinion incorrect. Samuel openly espoused Atterbury's cause, regardless of the consequences to himself. And there were consequences: Samuel lost his preferment and failed to be made Second Master of Westminster School, a position which was rightfully his after twenty years of outstanding service. This was a bitter disappointment to Mr. Wesley, and he was forced to content himself with the Head Mastership of the Blondell Free School at Tiverton, Devonshire. Here he served for seven years until his death, seven happy years in which he proved himself an able administrator as well as a superior teacher. He was "almost idolized" by the citizens of that place.

There was tragedy in the life of Samuel Wesley II. His wife presented him with a number of children, but only two lived to maturity. His son Samuel, who was the idol of his father, died quite young, leaving only a daughter called Phil to survive her parents.

Samuel Wesley, Jr. thoroughly disapproved of the Methodist movement and could never understand any part of it. He was a High Churchman to the core of his being and resented bitterly any slightest departure from the Church's stated forms and ways of doing things. In a letter to his mother on this subject, dated October, 1739, he writes: "For my own part, I had much rather have them [his brothers] picking straws within the walls than preaching in the area of Moorfields" (the Methodist center in London).

That his brothers, ordained clergymen of the Established Church, could preach out in the highways and the hedges and could substitute extempore prayers for the stately measures of the English Prayer Book was something he could not accept. He could never go along with their belief in the witness of the Spirit, and the stories that came to him of the emotional manifestations accompanying Methodist conversions were revolting to him.

Perhaps if Samuel had been in closer personal touch with his brothers during this period he would have been more tolerant, but this is doubtful. He was set in his ways, and High Churchmanship was a principle with him.

He bore no ill will toward John and Charles in all this matter, however. There was frank disagreement among them on the subject, and Samuel never hesitated to express his opinion; but there was never any diminution in the love and consideration the three brothers had for one another. Indeed, he commended the Methodists for the establishment of their

Charity School, and expressed the hope that John would build a church for the colliers (coal miners).

The last letter he ever wrote to John on the subject of Methodism, dated September 9, 1739, mentions the fact that he has been indisposed but adds: "I am on the mending hand in spite of foul weather." On November 5, 1739, he suddenly became very ill and died early the next morning. John and Charles were not informed of his death until after his burial, for in those days Devon was a long, long journey from London.

Perhaps the finest tribute to this stalwart character is these words which were part of the inscription carved on his grave stone in Tiverton church yard:

> An excellent preacher:
> But whose best sermon
> Was the constant example of an edifying life.

THE FOUNDERY . . . HAD A FINE LOCATION ON WINDMILL HILL.

12

SUSANNA at the FOUNDERY

Susanna's sons took the responsibility for their mother in settling up their father's affairs following his death. This had to be done as soon as possible in order to make way for the rector's successor to take possession of the rectory.

One of Samuel's fondest wishes was to pay his debts before he died, but it was unfulfilled. As he had requested, the rector was buried "very frugally, yet very decently," but he left a debt of about one hundred pounds and, in addition, another

151

fifteen pounds for rent due on a field which the family had
rented for pasture. On the day of Samuel's burial, the owner
of the field seized all their quick stock, valued at forty pounds,
for the fifteen pounds rent. John immediately paid the rental
fee, thus releasing the stock in order to allow his mother to
sell all to the greatest advantage.

It was John who now seems to assume the position as head
of the family. It was he—priest that he was—who had made
the commendatory prayer during his father's last moments,
and now it was John who helped his mother wind up all business matters before she left the Epworth parsonage forever.

She sold the stock, the farming equipment of every kind,
and all the furniture—everything she had in the world—to pay
what was owed. The sum remaining after all obligations had
been met cannot have been a large amount, because for the
rest of her days Susanna was dependent upon the bounty of
her children. They never failed her. Out of their own meager
incomes they cared for her with the tenderness that characterized Susanna's family through its entire history.

Samuel, Jr. was unable to reach Epworth before his father
died, but at his mother's urgent request he joined his brothers
there as they arranged for her final departure from the rectory.
To Samuel, her oldest son, she looked for whatever financial
help she must have, as is shown by a letter from Charles to his
older brother: "If you take London in your way [en route
to Epworth], my mother desires you will remember that she
is a clergyman's widow. Let the Society give her what they
please, she must be still, in some degree burdensome to you,
as she calls it. How do I envy you that glorious burden and
wish I could share it with you! You must put me in some
way of getting a little money, that I may do something in this
shipwreck of the family, though it be no more than furnishing
a plank!"

In that same letter Charles writes:

"It will be highly necessary to bring all accounts of what

he owed you, that you may mark all the goods in the house as principal creditor." The family was always in debt to Sammy!

Samuel, Jr. took sister Kezzy home with him, and Susanna went to live for a time with Emilia at her school in nearby Gainsborough. It is not illogical to suppose that Susanna readily entered into the life of Emilia's school. Certainly she herself had had long experience in teaching and had even taken a lively interest through letters in John's students at Oxford.

The year 1735 proved an eventful one for Susanna. In the summer of that year Martha was married to the Reverend Westley Hall. She was then living with her uncle Dr. Matthew Wesley in London and was married from his home and with his blessing. This was before the true character of Mr. Hall came to light. The happy couple took up residence in the rectory at Wooton.

One of the most notable events for Susanna during this year was the departure of her sons John and Charles for the colony of Georgia in America. This colony had been established by General Oglethorpe in 1733, primarily as a refuge for a group of his unfortunate countrymen who were languishing in English jails for debt. Samuel Wesley, as well as his oldest son, had been tremendously interested in this project; indeed, father Samuel had for many years expressed a longing to be a missionary himself. Both Samuels had made small personal contributions in money toward this enterprise and had sent as a gift the paten and chalice for administering the Sacrament in the new colony.

By 1735, General Oglethorpe had assembled a second group for emigration to Georgia, among them a company of persecuted Protestants from Bavaria, including a goodly number of Moravian Brethren. John Wesley was asked to join the group as their chaplain. He refused the invitation because of his obligation to take care of his widowed mother, but the

leaders of the company prevailed upon him to find out what
was Mrs. Wesley's opinion on this matter.

Her answer was characteristic: "Had I twenty sons, I should
rejoice that they were all so employed, though I should never
see them more." Charles Wesley was asked to go also as
secretary to General Oglethorpe—and a poor secretary he
turned out to be. Charles, because of the urgency of the
situation, was ordained immediately, first as deacon and then
as priest, and the company sailed from Gravesend on October
14, 1735.

In September of 1736, Susanna went to live with Sammy
at Tiverton where she enjoyed the company of her oldest son
and his wife and daughter, and also that of Mrs. Berry,
mother of Mrs. Samuel Wesley, Jr. It was understood that
John Wesley was to send home from Georgia to Samuel the
money for Kezzy's board, since Sammy was financially unable
to support both his mother and sister. Whether this money
was ever forthcoming is not known, but about this time Kezzy
went to live with the Halls.

In early December, 1736, Charles returned from Georgia,
discouraged over his mission and over his own spiritual state.
Shortly after his arrival he went to his brother Samuel's
house at Tiverton, and despite the fact that he found his
mother confined to her room because of illness, this homecoming was a singularly happy one.

During these later years Susanna did more traveling than
in all her married life put together. July of 1737 found her
with the Halls at Wooton, and she later moved with them to
Fisherton near Salisbury. These were pleasant months for
Susanna. Her health was better, and Martha and her husband
were most kind and hospitable to her. This was before Mr. Hall
fell into his evil ways.

During the same year John Wesley came back from Georgia
and, like Charles, he had a deep sense of failure. Though he
and Charles were later urged to return to America, Susanna

with her practical discernment saw that they were both better suited to be clergymen in England than missionaries to the Indians, and she persuaded them not to make a second journey to America.

The autumn of 1738 and the winter months following Susanna spent with Samuel. Little did she dream that this was to be her last stay with this beloved son on whom through many years she had relied more than upon her other children.

Susanna was becoming more and more infirm. In 1740, John took his mother to make her home with him in his newly established living quarters at the Methodist center in London known as the Foundery. Here she could be more comfortable than at any other place.

By this time the momentous event that Methodists call John Wesley's conversion had taken place in Aldersgate Street, and the Wesley who had come back from America discouraged and a failure was now the Wesley who was beginning to set all England on fire. The revival was already gathering momentum, and societies of "the people called Methodists" were being founded all about, with John Wesley the organizing genius and unquestioned leader. Charles Wesley had been converted three days before his brother John, and at once became an essential member of this itinerant partnership. He proved a powerful preacher and at this period was beginning his long career as the hymn writer par excellence.

John soon felt it essential to establish a London headquarters for Methodist work, but he lacked the funds for erecting such a building. With his customary ingenuity he conceived the idea of refurbishing for this purpose an old foundery, which had been formerly used for the casting of cannon. In 1716, a terrific explosion had ripped open a side of this building; since then it had been left unused. With the help of subscriptions and loans, Wesley secured the property for very little and adapted it to his purposes. The Foundery, as it continued to be called, had a fine location on Windmill Hill adjacent to

Moorfields, an expansive city park with lovely trees and grassy sward.

When Susanna came to the Foundery to live, she found an antiquated building ingeniously adapted to many uses. There was a crude chapel seating fifteen hundred people and a smaller meeting room with a capacity of three hundred seats. There was a Book Room also. In addition, the Foundery housed a Free School with two masters and sixty children; a Free Dispensary, the first in London since the dissolution of the monasteries; and living quarters for lay workers. There was also a coach house with a stable. Above the room where the Methodist "bands" met was John Wesley's apartment. Here Susanna lived for the remainder of her days, and here she died.

The Foundery offered Mrs. Wesley the happiest surroundings she had known for a long while. There was no longer the old struggle to provide food for a growing family, nor the eternal specter of debt. Here she had the companionship of John between the travels which his work required. Charles visited her often. Her daughters were all close by: Patty, Hetty in Soho, Anne now at Hatfield, and Kezzy at Bexley, boarding on the bounty of John and Charles with the family of the vicar, the Reverend Henry Piers, formerly a member of the Holy Club.

In the very early days following the conversion of John and Charles, Samuel Wesley, Jr. had made it clear that he was not in sympathy with his brothers' activities. Susanna then shared his views to an extent, though she always kept an open mind. At that time neither Susanna nor Samuel, Jr. had firsthand knowledge about the Methodist movement. The extraordinary dreams and visions and the highly emotional reactions of some of the Methodist converts were alarming to them both, steeped as they were in High Church tradition, and there was a rather indignant interchange of letters between them on this subject. The following excerpt from a letter written by Susanna. to her son Samuel is worthy of insertion. It is dated Thursday, March 8, 1738-39 (no place given) :

You have heard, I suppose, that Mr. Whitefield is taking a progress through these parts to make a collection for a house in Georgia for orphans and such of the natives' children as they will part with to learn our language and religion. He came hither to see me, and we talked about your brothers. I told him I did not like their way of living, wished them in some place of their own, wherein they might regularly preach, etc. He replied, "I could not conceive the good they did in London; that the greatest part of our clergy were asleep, and that there never was a greater need of itinerant preachers than now"; upon which a gentleman that came with him said that my son Charles had converted him, and that my sons spent their time in doing good. I then asked Mr. Whitefield if my sons were not for making some innovations in the Church, which I much feared. He assured me they were so far from it that they endeavoured all they could to reconcile Dissenters to our communion; that my son John had baptized five adult Presbyterians in our own way on St. Paul's day, and he believed would bring over many to our communion. His stay was short, so I could not talk with him so much as I desired. He seems to be a very good man, and one who truly desires the salvation of mankind. God grant that the wisdom of the serpent may be joined to the innocence of the dove! [1]

But when Susanna took up residence at the Foundery, she had opportunity to talk at length with John and Charles about their new-found religious experiences and about the work to which they were now dedicated, heart and soul. And when she came into close contact with the Methodists of London and saw at first hand their remarkable accomplishments, she was won over to the Methodist movement and found herself enthusiastically a part of it.

Not so with her son Samuel. Because of the great distance between Tiverton and London, he was never able to discuss this whole matter with his brothers face-to-face, though the three carried on a voluminous correspondence on the subject. Besides, Samuel was an entirely different type from his mother. He was more inflexible than she, and having once formed an opinion it was seldom that he could make any compromise whatever. He was intolerant of the Methodists till his dying day.

Mrs. Wesley is said to have taught classes of women at the Foundery. Certainly she was at the vortex of Methodist activity. Moreover, her sons as always continued to turn to their mother for advice and counsel on many phases of the tremendous undertaking to which they were now whole-heartedly committed. Each day she watched the progress of the various activities all about her. She sat under the preaching of her sons, and on one occasion accompanied John to Kennington Common and heard him preach to twenty thousand people. (The estimate of twenty thousand was John's, and his biographers tell us that he was notoriously prone to overestimate his crowds.) Furthermore, she was able to witness the revival fires, kindled by her sons, spreading with incredible swiftness over the British Isles—the revival predicted by her beloved husband near the end of his life. He never dreamed that his own family would have such a prominent part in the fulfillment of his prophecy.

In her new environment at the Foundery, so different from the staid atmosphere of the Church of England parish to which she was accustomed, Susanna Wesley furnished a striking demonstration of the breadth of vision which had really characterized her all along. Though accustomed to the stately ritual of the Church of England and all its rigid tenets, she was able, when an old lady, to adjust to the outdoor preaching of the Methodists, their extempore prayers, and all the innovations of their evangelistic fervor. Nor was Susanna's attitude one of mere resignation to something she could not control. She came to be convinced that the movement was of

God and a manifestation on a vast scale of that "inner witness" which her High Church husband had believed to be "the strongest proof of Christianity." After all, Susanna herself had made startling innovations when she thought such were right, her kitchen "preaching" not the least of them.

In late 1739, one of the greatest sorrows of Susanna's life came to her through the sudden death of her son Samuel. Strangely enough, John upon learning the news of his brother's passing, set off post haste for Tiverton without informing his mother of what had happened. She was none too well herself, and perhaps he feared the effect upon her.

A letter to Charles, written by Susanna on November 29, 1739, reveals some of her feelings:

Upon the first hearing of your brother's death, I did immediately acquiesce in the will of God, without the least reluctance. . . . Your brother was exceeding dear to me in this life, and perhaps I have erred in loving him too well. I once thought it impossible for me to bear his loss, but none know what they can bear till they are tried. . . . Surely the manifestation of His presence and favour is more than an adequate support under any suffering whatever. . . . I rejoice in having a comfortable hope of my dear son's salvation. . . . He hath reached the haven before me, but I shall soon follow him. . . .

I thank you for your care of my temporal affairs. It was natural to think that I should be troubled for my dear son's death on that account, because so considerable a part of my support was cut off. . . .

I cannot write much, being but weak. I have not been downstairs above ten weeks, though better than I was lately.[2]

This was a period of relative peace for Susanna. Regarding her own small financial needs, as she wrote her son Charles following Sammy's death: ". . . now our Heavenly Father seemed to have taken my cause more immediately into his own hand." And she was taking part in the activities at the

Foundery too. Indeed, at this juncture she performed one of the finest missions of her life. It came about in this fashion:

John Wesley knew himself called of God to be an evangelist, and his dynamic preaching was a proof of his calling. He had now started his tireless travels over England, Ireland, Scotland, and Wales, by boat, on foot, and on horseback, preaching and organizing Methodist Societies as he went. But the nurturing of these groups after they were begun was a serious problem, since the clergy in the various parishes did not come up to what he expected them to do.

Whenever John and Charles Wesley were away from the Foundery on their evangelistic missions, a layman named Thomas Maxfield was left in charge of the meetings of the Bands and of the Societies. Being a layman he was never permitted to preach; this right was reserved for the ordained clergy only. Maxfield might read the Scriptures and explain them. That was as far as he could go in the services. But on one occasion he dared to do an unprecedented thing: he *preached* to the congregation! When John Wesley got wind of this, he hurried back to London. The imperious leader of Methodism was in no good mood. Who was Thomas Maxfield to presume to take over the sacred function of preaching!

When John Wesley strode into the Foundery he was met by none other than Susanna. His face betrayed his marked displeasure, and his mother immediately inquired into the cause.

"Thomas Maxfield has turned preacher, I find," was his curt reply.

And here his mother took a stand which was to affect the whole course of Methodism. "John," she rejoined calmly, "you know what my sentiments have been. You cannot suspect me of favoring readily anything of this kind. But take care what you do with respect to that young man; for he is as surely called of God to preach as you are. Examine what have been the fruits of his preaching, and hear him yourself."

John was fair. He heard young Maxfield preach, and as he listened there remained no shadow of doubt in his mind but that his mother was right. "It is the Lord!" he said. "Let him do what seemeth him good. What am I that I should withstand God!"

Thus began lay preaching as a regularly constituted part of Methodist procedures. Its addition solved a difficult problem of organization in the fast multiplying Societies, for there were not nearly enough evangelistic preachers to go around. Many of the lay preachers, to be sure, were unlettered men, but they brought into the Methodist movement a spiritual virility that did much toward the spread of Methodism over the world.

In 1740, Emilia with her trusted servant joined her mother to live in John's apartment at the Foundery. Historians are vague as to whether her husband had died by this time, but it is certain that he furnished her no support. It was a comfort to Susanna to have Emilia with her in these latter days; this daughter had been on many occasions a strong arm for her mother to lean upon. As it came about, for many long years John took care of Emilia, first at the Foundery and later at the West Street Chapel after it had been added to the center. Her living quarters opened directly into the gallery behind the pulpit.

Incidentally, Emilia's apartment in West Street Chapel was the only real home John Wesley knew during those unhappy years of his ill-fated marriage.

Emilia's life was enthusiastically dedicated to the work of the Methodists until the infirmities of age prevented her leaving her room. Even then she could open the door of her bedroom and listen to the services in the Chapel below.

On the ninth of March, 1741, another sorrow came to Susanna in the death of Kezzy at Bexley. She had always been frail and was only thirty-two years of age when she died. Her brother Charles was the only member of the family at her bedside when she passed away.

Susanna's frailty was now becoming increasingly apparent to those who were associated with her from day to day. She suffered from no specific disease except gout, but her weary body was gradually giving way. She had never been robust in constitution, and the many hardships of her life and her frequent childbearing were contributing factors to this gradual decline. During these last years of her life she craved the companionship of her sons and daughters. Toward the end of 1739, she wrote to her son Charles that John's visits "are seldom and short, for which I never blame him, because I know he is well employed, and blessed be God, hath great success in his ministry. But, my dear Charles, still I want either him or you; for, indeed, in the most literal sense, I am become a little child and want continual succor."

More and more frequent now were the periods when she was confined to her bedroom. Here, alone, above the busy hum of the Foundery below, her room—had she wished it so—could have been peopled with poignant memories of those creative days in the Epworth Rectory—Samuel trudging off on his pastoral calls or incommunicado in his study, endlessly dictating the scholarly *Dissertations on the Book of Job;* baby Kezzy patting her tiny feet to scare away the ghost; the children in regimental order in the schoolroom, each at his appointed task; the tragic fire with John in the arms of the rescuing neighbor—John, the "brand plucked from the burning" for a mission that was now rapidly unfolding before her very eyes.

These were days of fulfillment for Susanna. Looking back over her eventful life, she could not fail to realize that the most important objective for which she had worked in the training of her children had been attained. She had always had a meticulous care for their education and their decorum, but the development of their character was the real goal of all her striving—and she had reached her goal. There was great misfortune for some of her children, especially her daughters, and unrelenting tragedy for a few. This she would have given her very life blood to avoid. But as the years unfolded, each of her children had measured up to what life brought and found the faith which was sufficient for all needs.

By early summer of 1742, Susanna's children were quite aware that the sands were running out for their mother, and they visited her as often as possible. The end came for Susanna on July 23, 1742. She was seventy-three years of age. Charles was forced to leave London on urgent business as the end approached and was not present at the last. All the other children were with her in her final hour, and John repeated the commendatory prayer for his mother just as he had seven years before for his father. They dutifully carried out her final request: "Children, as soon as I am released, sing a psalm of praise to God."

Susanna Wesley was buried in the Dissenters' cemetery, Bunhill Fields, across City Road from the site of what was later Wesley's Chapel. John read the service of the Church of England and beside her grave delivered a sermon to "almost an innumerable company of people" who were there to do her honor. Not far from her resting place in Bunhill Fields lies the body of John Bunyan; Isaac Watts is buried in the same cemetery, and also Susanna's sister, Elizabeth Dunton.

The mistress of the Epworth parsonage would never have been remembered at all except for the renown of her sons; yet in her own right she occupies an honored niche in history's hall of fame. Her claim to this distinction is as the successful mother of many children; all her other achievements are subordinate to that supreme function.

If only before the end of her troublous life she could have

had a look into the future to see a worldwide church whose founder was born to *her,* a poor parson's wife, in that modest parsonage on the dreary flats of Lincolnshire!

And if there could have been revealed to her the tremendous part played in all this by herself, Susanna Wesley, she would have refused to believe it—that it was her disciplined regimen of life that through her son John gave the very name to the people called Methodists; that it was from her that he inherited the logical mind and the singleness of purpose that characterized his leadership; that hers was, by all odds, the greatest influence in the life of that same son, John Wesley who, as William Fitchett expresses it, "represents the force which has most profoundly affected English history" in the eighteenth century.

No, the Susanna Wesley who wrote, "I am content to fill a little space if God be glorified," would never have deemed herself worthy of the place that history has accorded her.

SAYINGS
of SUSANNA

We must take the world as we find it, since it is a happiness permitted to very few to choose their company.

Take care of the world, lest it unawares steal away your heart.

Old age is the worst time we can choose to mend either our lives or our fortunes.

I am induced to believe that it is much easier to be contented without riches than with them.

You must not think to live like the rest of the world.

(To John regarding his preaching) Be very cautious in giving nice distinctions in public assemblies; for it does not answer the true end of preaching which is to mend men's lives and not fill their heads with unprofitable speculations.

Do not live like the rest of mankind, who pass through the world like straws upon a river, which are carried which way the stream or wind drives them.

A Christian ought, and in general does, converse with the world like a stranger in an inn; he will use what is necessary for him, and cheerfully enjoy what he innocently can; but at sometime he knows it is but an inn, and he will be but little concerned with what he meets with there, because he takes it not for his home.

The best preparation I know of for suffering is a regular and exact performance of present duty.

Make poetry sometimes your diversion, tho' never your business.

Whatever increases the strength and authority of your body over your mind, that thing is sin to you (however innocent it may be in itself).

Give God the praise for any well-spent day.

I am content to fill a little space if God be glorified.

NOTES

Chapter 1
  1. The Wesleys arrived at Epworth early in the year 1697.
  2. G. J. Stevenson, *Memorials of the Wesley Family*, pp. 71-72.
  3. Living, or, more properly, benefice: an ecclesiastical post or office to which property or a determined revenue is attached (a perpetual curacy). *See* Webster's *New International Dictionary, in loc. Benefice; see also,* New Schaff-Herzog, *Encyclopedia of Religious Knowledge.* Ed. Samuel Macaulay Jackson, 1908, *in loc. Benefice.*
  4. John Cuming Walters, *In Tennyson Land.*
  5. *See* Eliza Clarke, *Susanna Wesley,* p. 10.
  6. John Kirk, *The Mother of the Wesleys,* p. 64.

Chapter 2
  1. J. O. A. Clark, *The Wesley Memorial Volume,* p. 31.
  2. Abel Stevens, *The History of Methodism,* I, 43.
  3. Adam Clarke, *Memoirs of the Wesley Family,* I, 54-55.
  4. Frances Rose-Troup, *John White, Patriarch of Dorchester and the Founder of Massachusetts, 1575-1648,* XII, 483.

Chapter 3
1. Adam Clarke, *Memoirs of the Wesley Family,* I, 128.
2. Harvey Graham, *Eternal Eve, the History of Gynaecology and Obstetrics,* Chap. XI, p. 269.
3. William H. Fitchett, *Wesley and His Century,* p. 141.
4. John Richard Green, *Nations of the World: England,* IV, 127.
5. William H. Fitchett, *Wesley and His Century,* p. 139.
6. Thomas Babington Macaulay, *History of England,* I, 305-7.
7. John Richard Green, *Nations of the World: England,* IV, 137.

Chapter 4
1. William H. Fitchett, *Wesley and His Century,* p. 31.
2. Adam Clarke, *Memoirs of the Wesley Family,* II, 132, 133.
3. V. H. H. Green, *The Young Mr. Wesley,* p. 50; quoting from *John Wesley's Parents,* by Robert Walmsley, in *Proceedings of the Wesley Historical Society,* XXIX, 50-57.
4. *See* John Kirk, *The Mother of the Wesleys,* p. 143.
5. *Ibid.,* pp. 121-22.

Chapter 5
1. "Pilfering," says Dr. Maldwyn Edwards, probably meant "playing" obviously the word did not mean "stealing."
2. Eliza Clarke, *Susanna Wesley,* pp. 29-36. Adam Clarke also gives Susanna's "Method" in its entirety: *Memoirs of the Wesley Family,* II, 9-15.

Chapter 6
1. Luke Tyerman, *The Life and Times of the Reverend Samuel Wesley,* p. 353.
2. Adam Clarke, *Memoirs of the Wesley Family,* I, 272.
3. *Ibid.,* I, 265.

Chapter 7
1. Convocation: A national assembly of the clergy meeting by royal order contemporaneously with the sessions of Parliament. Each Convocation had two Houses: the Upper House composed of bishops and the Lower House made up of deans, archbishops, and proctors representing the clergy of the various dioceses. The actions of these gatherings were formerly of great importance but were shorn of much of their power after the reign of Henry VIII. It was Convocation that revised the *Book of Common Prayer,* completed in 1661, giving rise to the famous Act of Uniformity of 1662.
2. Maldwyn Edwards, *Family Circle,* pp. 5-6.
3. Adam Clarke, *Memoirs of the Wesley Family,* I, 389-90.

Chapter 8

1. Luke Tyerman, *The Life and Times of the Reverend Samuel Wesley,* p. 402.
2. Eliza Clarke, *Susanna Wesley,* pp. 138-39.
3. Luke Tyerman, *The Life and Times of the Reverend Samuel Wesley,* p. 419.
4. *Ibid.,* p. 391.
5. Eliza Clarke, *Susanna Wesley,* p. 143.
6. Adam Clarke, *Memoirs of the Wesley Family,* II, 79-80.
7. There were no examinations at Oxford in John Wesley's day for candidates for a Bachelor of Arts degree; so the College each year appointed a moderator of classes as well as a Greek lecturer. The former presided over instruction in logic and philosophy.
8. Luke Tyerman, *The Life and Times of the Reverend Samuel Wesley,* p. 436.

Chapter 9

1. V. H. H. Green, *The Young Mr. Wesley,* p. 42.
2. Luke Tyerman, *The Life and Times of the Reverend Samuel Wesley,* p. 427.
3. *See* Adam Clarke, *Memoirs of the Wesley Family,* II, 262-64.
4. *Ibid.,* II, 322.

Chapter 10

1. G. J. Stevenson, *Memorials of the Wesley Family,* p. 298.
2. *Ibid.,* p. 302.
3. V. H. H. Green, *The Young Mr. Wesley,* p. 109.
4. Unfortunately, this letter has been lost. George Stephenson reports having seen it as well as an abridgment of it made by John Wesley.
5. John Kirk, *The Mother of the Wesleys,* p. 202.
6. Eliza Clarke, *Susanna Wesley,* p. 136.
7. Adam Clarke, *Memoirs of the Wesley Family,* II, 290-93.
8. *The Arminian Magazine,* I, 187-88 (London ed. for the year 1778).
9. William H. Fitchett, *Wesley and His Century,* p. 36.
10. A. T. Quiller-Couch, *Hetty Wesley,* p. 142.
11. G. J. Stevenson, *Memorials of the Wesley Family,* p. 306.
12. *Ibid.,* p. 315.

Chapter 11

1. Adam Clarke, *Memoirs of the Wesley Family,* II, 237.
2. Eliza Clarke, *Susanna Wesley,* p. 151.

Chapter 12

1. G. J. Stevenson, *Memorials of the Wesley Family,* p. 216.
2. *Ibid.,* pp. 218-19.

BIBLIOGRAPHY

Ashton, John. *Social Life in the Reign of Queen Anne*. London: Chatto & Windus, 1911.

Barry, Iris. *Portrait of Lady Mary Montagu*. Indianapolis: Bobbs-Merrill, 1928.

Brailsford, Mabel R. *Susanna Wesley: the Mother of Methodism*. London: Epworth Press, 1938.

Brailsford, Mabel R. *A Tale of Two Brothers: John and Charles Wesley*. London: Rupert Hart-Davis, 1954.

Churchill, Winston (American) *Richard Carvel*. New York & London: The Macmillan Co., 1899.

Clark, Elmer T. *An Album of Methodist History*. New York & Nashville: Abingdon-Cokesbury Press, 1952.

Clark, J. O. A. *The Wesley Memorial Volume*. New York: Phillips & Hunt, 1880.

Clarke, Adam. *Memoirs of the Wesley Family*. 2 vol., 2nd. rev. ed., London: W. Tegg, 1836

Clarke, Eliza. *Eminent Women Series: Susanna Wesley*. Ed. John H. Ingram. 2nd. ed., London: W. H. Allen & Co., 1890.

Clendening, Logan, M., ed. *A Source Book of Medical History*. New York and London: Paul B. Hoeber, 1942.

Edwards, Maldwyn. *Family Circle; a Study of the Epworth House-hold in Relation to John and Charles Wesley.* London: Epworth Press, 1949.

———, *John Wesley and the Eighteenth Century.* London: George Allen and Unwin, Ltd., 1933.

Fitchett, Wm. H. *Wesley and His Century.* New York, Cincinnati: Abingdon Press, 1917.

Fitzgerald, O. P. *Eminent Methodists.* Chap. on Susanna Wesley by Bishop C. B. Galloway. Publishing House of The Meth. Episcopal Church, South; Nashville, Tenn., 1896.

Flint, Bishop Charles Wesley. *Charles Wesley and his Colleagues.* Washington, D.C.: Public Affairs Press, 1957.

Graham, Harvey; pseud. (Isaac Flack). *Eternal Eve, The History of Gynaecology and Obstetrics.* Garden City, New York: Doubleday, 1951.

Green, John Richard. *England.* Vol. IV. New York: Peter Fenelon Collier & Son, 1900. (Part of a Series called *Nations of the World.*)

Green, V. H. H. *The Young Mr. Wesley.* New York: St. Martin's Press, Inc., 1961.

Haddal, Ingvar. *John Wesley.* Nashville: Abingdon Press, 1961.

Hall, Walter Phelps & Albion, Robert Greenhalgh. *A History of England and the British Empire.* Boston: Ginn & Co., 1953.

Harrison, Grace Elizabeth. *Son to Susanna.* Nashville: Cokesbury Press, 1938.

Johnson's England. Ed. A. S. Turberville. Oxford: Clarendon Press, 1933.

King, Lester S., M.D. *The Medical World of the Eighteenth Century.* Chicago: The University of Chicago Press, 1958.

Kirk, John. *The Mother of the Wesleys.* Cincinnati: Poe & Hitchcock, 1867.

Lecky, W. E. H. A. *A History of England in the Eighteenth Century.* London: Longman's, Green, 1925.

Marshall, Dorothy. *Eighteenth Century England.* London: Longman's, 1962.

Maser, Frederick E. *Susanna Wesley.* Published by the Association of Methodist Historical Societies, Lake Junaluska, N.C., 1962?

McConnell, Francis John. *John Wesley.* Nashville: Abingdon Press, 1939.

Priestley, Joseph. *Original Letters by the Reverend John Wesley and His Friends.* Birmingham, England: Thomas Pearson, 1791.

Quennell, Marjorie and C. H. B. *A History of Everyday Things in England.* London: Batsford, 1938.

Quiller-Couch, A. T. *Hetty Wesley.* London: The Amalgamated Press, Ltd., n.d.

Snowden, Rita F. *Such a Woman; the Story of Susanna Wesley.* Nashville: The Upper Room, 1962.

Stephen, Sir Leslie. *English Literature and Society in the Eighteenth Century.* Ford Lectures. New York: G. P. Putnam's Sons, 1907.

Stevens, Abel. *The History of the Religious Movement of the Eighteenth Century, Called Methodism.* Vol. I. New York: Carlton & Porter, 1858.

Stevenson, George J. *Memorials of the Wesley Family.* London: S. W. Partridge & Co., 1867.

Teeter, Herman B. "Mother of Methodism," *Together Magazine,* April, 1958.

Traill, A. D. *Social England.* Vol. IV. London, Paris & Melbourne: Cassell & Co., 1895.

Trevelyan, George Macaulay. *England Under Queen Anne-Blenheim.* London: Longmans, Green & Co., 1959.

———, *Illustrated English Social History.* Vols. II & III. London: Longmans, Green & Co., 1958.

Tyerman, Luke. *The Life and Times of the Reverend John Wesley.* 3 vols. New York: Harper & Brothers, 1872.

———, *The Life and Times of the Reverend Samuel Wesley, M.A., Rector of Epworth.* London: Simpkin, Marshall & Co., 1866.

Walters, John Cuming. *In Tennyson Land.* London: George Redway, 1890.

Wesley, John *The Journal of the Reverend John Wesley.* Ed. Nehemiah Curnock. 8 vols. London: Epworth Press, 1938.

———, *Letters of the Reverend John Wesley.* Ed. John Telford. London: Epworth Press, 1931.

Wilson, Woodrow. *John Wesley's Place in History.* New York & Cincinnati: Abingdon Press, 1915.

INDEX

Act of Uniformity, 26
Aldersgate Street, 155
Anglesea, Earl of, 27
Anne, Queen, 32
Annesley, Anne, 18
Annesley, Benjamin, 18
Annesley, Elizabeth (Dunton), 18, 163
Annesley, Judith, 18
Annesley, Dr. Samuel, 16, 18-19, 24-25; characterization of, 27-28
Annesley, Mrs. Samuel, 28
Annesley, Samuel, Jr., 17, 45, 54; mysterious disappearance of, 87-88
Annesley, Sarah, 18
Anslye, John (grandfather of Susanna), 24
Anslye, Judith (grandmother of Susanna), 24
Arminian Magazine, The, 71, 73, 130
Athenian Gazette, The, 34, 41-42

Atterbury, Bishop Francis, 146, 148
Attkins, Will, 119
Axholme, "Isle of," 15-16

Baker, Frank, 10, 30, 122-23
Berkeley, Bishop George, 37
Berry, Mrs. John (mother-in-law of Samuel Wesley, Jr.), 154
Bexley, 115, 156, 161
Black Raven Printing Establishment, 22
Bristol, 136, 143; Charles Wesley settles there, 143
Brown, John, 99
Brown, Robin, 67, 70
Bunhill Fields, 163
Butler, Bishop Joseph, 37

Caroline, Queen, 100
Castleton, Lord, 42
Chamberlens (practitioners of obstetrics), 36
Charles I, King, 25

173

Charles II, King, 26; court of, 32-33, 39
Charterhouse School, 56, 81
City Road Chapel, 143
Clarke, Adam, quoted, 24, 30, 44
Coffee houses, 33-34
Convocation, 46-47, 77, 80, 82

Divine right of kings, 82
Dorchester Free School, 21
Dunton, John, 21, 41

Ellison, Richard, 108-9
Epworth Rectory, 51, 66; description of, 14-15; visit of Archbishop Sharpe to, 50; burned, 51-54
Epworth, town of, 43, 48-49, 54, 65

Five Mile Act, 29
Foundery, the, 155-58
Fuller, Thomas, 30

Gainsborough, town of, 46, 153
Genealogical table of the Wesleys, 6-7
Gentleman's Magazine, The, 110
Georgia, Colony of, 143, 153-55
Grantham, Mr. and Mrs., 119

Hall, Westley, 112-13
Hall, Westley, Jr., 112-13, 140
Harper, Robert, 107-8
Haxey, parish register of, 123
Holborn (London), 41
Holy Club, 139, 141
Hoole, Joseph, 69

Inman, The Rev. Mr. (curate), 77-78, 80
Job, Dissertations on the Book of, 93, 97-100

Johnson, Samuel, 65, 113

Kelstein, 119
Kennington Common, 158
Kingswood School, 63
"Kitchen preaching," 78-80

Lambert, John, 110
Leybourne, Robert, 107
Lincoln Castle (prison), 49, 50
Lincoln, College of Oxford, 90-91, 94
Lincolnshire, 39
Little St. Helen's, 17, 27
Louth, 121, 123-24

Macaulay, Lord, quoted, 38
Mary, Queen, 42-43
Marylebone churchyard, 144
Massy, Betty, 70
Maxfield, Thomas, 160-61
Method of education (Susanna's), 57-65
Montagu, Lady Mary Wortley, 34

Normanby, Marquis of, 42-43

Oglethorpe, James, 153-54
Oxford, Lord, 147
Oxford Prison, 22, 140
Oxford University, 21, 82-83

Potter, John, Bishop of Oxford, 89

Romley, John, 111, 118

St. Andrews, parish of (Epworth), 43
St. Bartholomew's Day, 27
St. Giles, Anglican parish of, 17
School, Mrs. Taylor's, 94
Sharpe, John, Archbishop of York, 46, 50
Soho (London), 126, 156
South Ormsby, 13, 15, 41-43
Spital Yard, 17
Sprat, Bishop Thomas, 145

Tiverton, 148, 154

Vermuyden, Cornelius, 16, 48

Wesley, Anne or Nancy (Lambert), 44, 88, 110
Wesley, Bartholomew, 28, 30

Wesley, Charles, 51, 109, 126, 137, 159, 162; characterization of, 141-42; relation with John, 141-43; goes to Georgia, 153-54; as hymn writer, 144

Wesley, Charles (son of Charles), 142

Wesley, Elizabeth (Dyer), 20, 75

Wesley, Emilia (Harper), 54, 83-84, 105, 106-8, 153, 161; opinion on the ghost, 71; bemoans father's impractical ways, 86-87

Wesley, Garrett, 90

Wesley, John, 44, 57, 100-101, 109; saved from the fire, 53; interest in the ghost, 72-73; attends Charterhouse School, 81; ordained, 89; Fellow of Lincoln, 90-91; assists father in parish, 91-93; disagrees with father over Hetty, 124-25; characterization of, 139-41; brings mother to Foundery, 155; begins Methodist movement, 155-56

Wesley, John (father of Samuel), 20, 29-30

Wesley, Mrs. John (mother of Samuel), 30, 75

Wesley, Kezziah or Kezzy, 54, 75, 114-15, 161-62

Wesley, Martha or Patty (Hall), 51, 110-14, 153

Wesley, Mary or Molly (Whitelamb), 42, 97-98, 109-10, 120

Wesley, Matthew, 20, 30, 37, 39, 54; visits Epworth, 94-96

Wesley, Mehetabel or Hetty (Wright), 52, 54, 110, 117-37; connection with the ghost, 70; elopement, 88; correspondence with father, 131-33

Wesley, Phil (daughter of Samuel, Jr.), 149

Wesley, Sally or Sarah (daughter of Charles), 142

Wesley, Samuel (husband of Susanna), childhood, 20-21; student days, 18, 20-21, 40; characterization of, 43-44, 47-48; imprisoned for debt, 49-51; unforgiveness toward Hetty, 120-21, 124-25, 131-33; death of, 100-101; writings of, 22, 41-42, 45, 76, 100

Wesley, Samuel, Jr., 90, 123; education, 51, 55; 145-46; characterization of, 145-48; opposed to Methodism, 149-50, 156-58

Wesley, Samuel (son of Charles), 142

Wesley, Samuel Sebastian (grandson of Charles), 145

Wesley, Sarah (wife of Charles), 142-43

Wesley, Susanna or Sukey (Ellison, daughter of Susanna), 42, 54, 108-9

Wesley, Timothy, 20, 75

Wesley, Ursula (wife of Samuel, Jr.), 133, 146

Westminster School, 51, 56, 145

Whitchurch, 20, 29

White, John (grandfather of Susanna), 24

White, John (grandfather of Samuel), 30

Whitefield, George, 142, 157

Whitelamb, John, 97-98

William of Orange, King, 47

Wright, Amelia, 134

Wright, William, 121, 124, 126-30, 135, 137

Writings of Susanna, 15, 20, 76, 82, 92-93

Wroot, 85-86